SEEKERS OF A
STABLE SKY

STORIES OF ALTRUISM
AND IMMIGRATION
ON THE
MEXICAN BORDER

SEEKERS OF A STABLE SKY

STORIES OF ALTRUISM AND IMMIGRATION ON THE MEXICAN BORDER

ELAINE HAMPTON

with collaborators:
DRA. SAN JUANA MENDOZA, INEZ,
CUCA, MINERVA, ANAY POLOMEQUE,
GRECIA OROZCO, LINABEL SARLAT,
AND ELVIA VILLESCAS

atmosphere press

TABLE OF CONTENTS

~ 1 ~

THE ALLEGORICAL
FAULT LINE

Ciudad Juárez is a harsh city in the desert on the Mexican side of the U.S. border. Under the belly of that harshness, however, is a gentle, hidden, counter power led by women who have been wounded, crossed the border illegally, fought for their families, and endured consequences of social and economic exploitation while building caring communities. This authentic insight into the often-misrepresented immigrant narrative stems from accounts of global neighbors managing stressful environments, often hoping to enter the United States to have a more stable life.

I live thirty miles directly north of the Mexican border in Las Cruces, New Mexico, and for most of my life I have been able to cross easily. It started when I was a child in the 1960s. My dad would load the six of us in the car and drive over the bridge, crossing the dry Rio Grande. We bought groceries in the Mexican market. We watched the glass blowers in the glass factories turn used cola bottles into drinking glasses, vases, and intricate, tiny sailing ships made of strings of molten glass. We visited the downtown plaza to buy Mexican popsicles and play in the shade in front of the old church, built in 1659 by the Spanish priests overseeing the local indigenous peoples' (often forced) labor. It was cool inside those thick adobe walls. We were often the only White family around, and we received attention from informal vendors hoping to sell sweets or trinkets and some Mexicans who wanted to practice speaking English. There was always music in the streets, little boys or old men strumming a guitar or squeezing an accordion.

The energy and wonder that I felt in Mexico fascinated me, and I have continually looked to connect with the people of Mexico. I visit occasionally with a friend in Guadalajara and travel to see the country's natural wonders. I collaborated with professors at the university in Ciudad Juárez on environmental education projects. And, for a year, I hosted a family who fled extreme danger in their small community near Ciudad Juárez. They had a farm and a home. The United States decided to build a bridge across the river that would end near their farm. Unethical men saw the new value in that land and tortured, kidnapped, and later killed two men in the family to force their point. The rest of the family fled across the border and were eventually granted permission to stay.

In 2001, I had the opportunity to visit a church in Ciudad Juárez. There I met Anay. She was nineteen years old, the wife of a man seeking to be a preacher. They lived in a small room in the back of the church. She had a cute little baby, and she let me hold her during the church service. Eva started fussing, so Anay and I took her out to walk in the dirt road in front of the church. Anay's first words to me were, "I am really smart. I want to get my education. I am finishing my junior high school now. I am

4

really good in math. Come here. I'll show you my math work." We went into the small room in the corner of the church complex that served as their home. I sat on the mattress with Eva and her soggy diaper. Anay brought her workbook for math and showed me her good grades. She found a diaper and changed Eva. "Do you think you and your friends could get me thirty-five dollars every month so I can buy diapers for Eva?"

"Gutsy girl," I thought. "The only way I can get money across the border is to bring it every month. Well, I do like to visit Mexico. Now I know the way to get to this church. Thirty-five dollars is no problem."

"Sure. I can do that." And we have met at least every month since that day. We became dear friends. I knew our friendship was influenced by her dependence on my ability to give through my American abundance. But she paid me back in eye-opening experiences about real life on the Mexican border and beyond. With small support from me and giant energy and determination from her, she accomplished university education, a beautiful family, and a stable life.

I got to witness her struggle to get to that stable life. She and her husband, with support from a church friend in Texas, built a little house in a very low-income area in the desert sand hills on the south side of Ciudad Juárez. The time I spent with her there exposed a painful contrast between my life of privilege and her struggle to survive. An easy task for me took layers and layers of, often dangerous, effort to accomplish.

I drove my air-conditioned car to her house. She walked through the sand, down a busy highway, with (then) three young children to buy food and drinking water at the nearest store. I turned the tap and had fresh water. She went to a concrete tank in front of the house and scooped up clean, not potable, water; and poured it over the babies for their bath, washed with it using a scrub board, or boiled it to cook the meal – if they could afford to pay the water-delivery truck driver at the moment he came to their neighborhood. My home was climate controlled. They had a floor fan for the hot summer and a space heater, run by pirated electricity when available, for the coldest days. There was a ten-day stretch when a summer rainstorm flooded their neighborhood. The water receded to knee-level after a few days and her husband waded to the highway and then to the nearest convenience store for drinking water for the family. His only complaint to me was, "Phew. We were sure smelly those days."

North of the river, children ride school buses to a safe school with abundant learning materials and well-trained teachers. Anay and her husband once had a donated car, and, until it fell apart, she could drive it if her husband pushed it down the hill to the main street to get the car started. Then she drove her children to school. If the car didn't work, she walked the two miles to and from the school or rode a city bus if it went in the right direction. Because her husband received support from the U.S. church, their front room was the local church. And the neighbors, mostly with fewer resources than Anay's family, saw that as a source for clean water, nice used clothing donated from the U.S. friends, a ride to town when needed, and a free Sunday meal. They shared their resources and sometimes went without.

Her brother was assassinated, and her sister raped by the desperation that poverty delivers. She has endured robberies and avoided at least three kidnappings. She guards her children carefully.

Throughout these years, she was going to school to finish her junior high program, then high school, and then beauty school, the only available option for her at that time. She eventually graduated from an online program with a bachelor's degree in international business – with highest honors.

Yet, my restful nights were over. For those twenty years, I have lain in my comfortable bed, covered by my comfortable life, wide awake. My mind goes to Anay and the other women I met, and the struggle-of-the-hour that they are enduring, hopefully successfully, and my poor ability to understand, much less, intervene.

ACROSS THE DRY RIVER

That river that separates us, almost 2000 miles in length, begins in the mountains of Colorado and eventually forms the entire border between Texas and Mexico. Throughout history, she has brought life to this harsh desert region, meandering at leisure as she claimed her domain, sometimes drying up and sometimes raging in flooding torrents, leaving swampy lands and fertile plains.

The river is now colonized, bound up in dams, over-allocated, unequally distributed, and forced into engineered channels so her precious resources are diverted to serve those with powerful voices and full wallets. Her once massive reign is now a tightly controlled ditch marking the irritated and feverish political border line between two nations.

On the U.S. side of the Rio Grande is El Paso, Texas, with just under a million living in the city and nearby. The sandy hills and rocky mountainsides of west El Paso host pampered, well-planned and well-watered neighborhoods where homes and business are landscaped, roads are maintained, and well-engineered drain systems protect most areas from flooding and erosion when the summer monsoons detonate. Water to these homes is inexpensive and available at the touch of a tap.

On the Mexican side is Ciudad Juárez, home to about one and a half million people, many of whom are there to respond to siren calls from their northern neighbors' demand for cheap labor and drugs.

A thin, heavily reinforced borderline separates the cities, but family, friends, business, education, and entertainment weld them back together. For most of the region's history, its people crossed into and out of each city with ease, relishing two languages, two cultures, and two nations. Political impositions have slowed the flow; they have not stopped it.

Today, this border zone is more of an allegorical fault line where the world's richest nation scrapes against a younger democracy trying to survive tremors from extreme economic contrasts, heightened in recent history by a surge of foreign factories bringing hyper-exploitation through the abuse of unfair wages and fostering a caustic restructuring of Mexican society.

The stories in this book begin in Inez's community, Anapra, a neighborhood in the far northwest corner of Ciudad Juárez. A small mountain, Mount Cristo Rey, dominates Anapra's northern horizon and marks the location where Mexico, New Mexico, and Texas come together. A forty-two-foot statue of Jesus on a large cross with his arms spread wide sits atop the mountain. He faces El Norte. His back is turned to the Mexican side.

Anapra is built in sandy hills and rocky mountainsides crossed with deep arroyos. Rutted trails meet the paved roads, forming a grid for small homes – most of which are built of concrete block. A few homes are surrounded with ingenious fence designs such as old mattress springs standing up right and wired together. Mesquite shrubs that once covered the hills were plucked and burned for firewood decades ago. Used laundry water may sustain a rose bush or a small tree struggling against the dry winds and heat. Scrubby plants with plastic bags stuck in the thorns are common sights.

The community's beauty is not on the surface.

Anapra was formed in the 1980s as the North American Free Trade Agreement (NAFTA) facilitated economic interchanges, and non-Mexican corporations-built factories in Mexico, mostly located close to the border, easing transport of goods to the U.S. markets. In the United States, the factory workers would receive $10.00 to $20.00 per *hour*. The people working in factories just one or two miles south the U.S. border receive $5.00 to $10.00 per *day.* Workers do receive benefits, although at a much lower rate than U.S. workers, so corporations reap a great reduction in labor costs. From my experiences, the cost of many necessities in this area of Mexico is only slightly lower than in the United States. Stretching that small salary is difficult.

Those factories are called maquiladoras. It is a rare word in Spanish, pulled out of an old process for milling grain, and it is pronounced MA-**KEE**-LA-DORA. In the

1990s, maquiladora development exploded all along the Mexican side of the border. Thousands of Mexicans from the interior moved north to fill the jobs. The border cities could not meet those sudden demands for social infrastructure: water, transportation, schools, health care, childcare, and housing.

Many aspects of Mexican life were ravaged. For example, corn. Almost every Mexican farm produces corn, vital to Mexican way of life and sacred to native peoples. With NAFTA, Mexican stores now stock corn from the United States, which, because of government subsidies, is cheaper than Mexican-grown corn. Mexico lost a million jobs in corn alone. In the following years, undocumented immigration from Mexico, a desperate response to this and other effects of NAFTA, doubled.[1]

Anapra's residents are mostly from the interior of the country. They traveled north with the hope of eventually crossing into the Promised Land, and, in the meantime, to work in the maquiladoras. Most factories in this area are outreaches of U.S. corporate giants such as Delphi, Lexmark, Lear, Honeywell, and Boeing. As of 2020, there were some 330 factories and 250,000 employees in the Ciudad Juárez area alone. The factory workers make products vital to the U.S. consumer: computers, printers, parts for cars, heaters, vacuum cleaners, big screen televisions, and even blades for the giant wind turbines.

At the New Mexico border crossing just west of El Paso, there are a few factories making metal products and

---

[1] Rick Relinger. NAFTA and U.S. Corn Subsidies: Explaining the Displacement of Mexico's Corn Farmers. April 19, 2010. *Prospect Journal.*

packing materials on the U.S. side, and the giant Foxconn, a Chinese factory making computers, is the dominant structure on the Mexican side.

After entering Mexico, the eight-mile trip to Anapra is on a well-paved boulevard heading east and hugging the infamous border wall, built with funds from the George W. Bush administration. A heavy metal mesh fence allows a view into the U.S. desert with border patrol agents in pick-ups and four-wheelers ever vigilant for suspicious activity. Nearer Anapra, the wall is topped with five-foot tall heavy metal plates. Large white letters are painted on this metal edge in a clear, graffiti-art style, English and Spanish mixed, saying, *"Somos trabajadoras internecionales. Fuck Trump and his pinche mural."* [We are international workers. Fuck Trump and his pussy border wall.]

THE SCHOOL IN THE SAND

When I started my tenure at The University of Texas at El Paso in 1999, I became friends with a custodian, Emma, who sometimes stopped in my office for a short visit. Emma had been a teacher in Ciudad Juárez before she immigrated. Her teaching credentials did not qualify her to teach in the United States. "I never thought I would be a custodian. But I get paid much more here than in Mexico. My kids are in good schools. Here. You can see them." She opened the heart-shaped pendant around her neck guarding a picture of three smiling children. "When they are naughty, I turn the pendant backwards and they know they are in trouble." She laughed.

One day she saw a stack of notebooks on the shelf in my office. "If you have extra school supplies, there is a new school starting outside of Ciudad Juárez, in Anapra. They need everything."

I had been studying Spanish over the years, and by this time, I could manage conversations about familiar topics. I told her I would gather the needed school supplies if she would take me to that school. We went the next week. It was easier to cross then, and I was comfortable driving my car across the border. The last stretch of the path to the emerging elementary school was a sandy trail with giant potholes and sand traps, but we made it.

When we arrived, we saw a school in the sand, walls crafted of packing pallets and tar paper to accommodate some forty elementary children in the one small room. The parents had built this school. The teacher taught by standing in the corner giving a lecture as he wrote his lesson notes with one hand on a large tablet of chart paper held with his other hand.

An abandoned school bus was parked on the school lot. That eventually became the second classroom which was functional for three years before the city and state put money into building a better school.

The next year, during June, the teacher who was also serving as principal was teaching older students in that bus while trying to arrange graduation and end-of-school paperwork. I had taught science to sixth graders for nine years. I volunteered to take over his class-in-a-bus for a few days so he could get his work done. It was a thrill. The children and I had to be careful not to step in the hole with its rough metal edges. And we kept all the windows open, a small shove against the desert heat.

I had prepared a science lesson to grow a bean seed supported by a moist paper towel inside a small plastic bag. We would observe, document, and then design experiments to determine the best variables to support our little seedlings.

I brought a plastic jug of water and set it on the wobbly table. It was difficult to measure the water without the right equipment. Most of the students put too much water in their plastic bags. That would prevent the growth of their beans, so I told them (well, I thought I told them) they should only moisten the paper towel. They needed to pour the excess water out the bus windows onto the sand. They looked at me with wide eyes, glanced around at each other, and they all threw their baggies out the window.

On a different trip to the school in Anapra, I took a few of my university students with me. We brought candy. There was no way to distribute the candy equally, so when we left, the children who did not get any candy chased my car down the road as we drove away in humiliation.

Some friends heard about my visits and volunteered to clean out their closets so I could take the clothes and shoes over to the community. I collected a pick-up load of large plastic bags filled with used clothing. I never looked inside the bags; and I did not have the foresight to at least sort and label the donations.

At the school, there was a group of about twenty parents waiting for the clothes. People started dragging the bags out of the back of the pick-up and ripping them open. Chaos reigned, and I still have stuck in my mind the mothers standing in the sand digging large-sized, strappy high heels out of the bag and laughing at me. They could see the humor in a petite Mexican woman trying to walk the rutted roads in those heels; and they rightfully saw my impolite ignorance of their needs.

The school's kind principal did not give up on me. I apologized. He suggested we bring books to start a library. Have you ever read *Alexander and the Terrible, Horrible, No Good, Very Bad Day*? Cute book about a little kid who has trouble: woke up one morning with gum in his hair, tripped on a skateboard, sweater got wet, didn't get a toy in his breakfast cereal, too hot bath water, wrong seat in the car pool, didn't have the best drawing in his classroom with his nice teacher, and didn't get a cupcake in his lunch. Even in Spanish, I just could not give that book to a school where children did not have beds, skateboards, sweaters, bathtubs, breakfast, cars, schoolrooms, or cupcakes.

So, I learned to screen the books.

By 2008, the school regularly welcomed my university students to lead science learning activities in their class-rooms. Most of my students were bilingual, so language was no barrier.

Over these years, the city officials had been providing more funding to the school, and it was extended to ten classrooms. One wing had concrete floors; the other wing was still built on the sand. About 35 to 40 students were in each classroom. We brought books every time we visited, and I scraped up a little money to pay one of the mothers to manage the library. However, I had to urge my university students to control their desire to take gifts to the children. We were there to learn from each other, and trinkets and candy sent the wrong message. My students rated the cross-border teaching as one of the best university learning experiences.

By 2010, the city had provided more support to the

school and the facility was adequate with bathrooms, a covered playground, and three wings of classrooms.

Sadly, in the years around 2009, the violence in Ciudad Juárez escalated. Gang violence, corrupt leaders, and corrupt military filled the vacuum of social structures left in NAFTA's wake. Murders rose to eight per day. The school's director asked me not to come to Anapra anymore, for his and my safety. I quit crossing into Mexico. [Eventually, political and social organizations in Ciudad Juárez worked together and created a safer space – yet, still fragile and struggling to confront the effects of economic and social marginalization.]

I lost touch with the Anapra school and its community until 2017, when, at the farmers market near my home in Las Cruces, I saw a booth with strings of bright flags like the prayer flags that hang near Buddhist temples. These flags were covered with illustrations and wise sayings about peace, birthdays, New Mexico, *Amor por Juárez*, yoga, the Virgin Mary, and quotes from famous philosophers. The woman in charge of the booth, Sara, shared a flyer about these Guerilla Prayer Flags; they were made in Anapra by women who had children with severe disabilities. Profits from the sale of the prayer flags help the families purchase diapers, wheelchairs, medicine, therapy, and much more. These women also help other families in the neighborhood who have children with disabilities.

The flyer explained that the women worked in a small workshop in the back of a private lot to create and package the bright strings of cloth. Sara brought the finished flags to the U.S. to sell them at events and online venues. She told me that the prayer flag cooperative did not want much publicity in the Ciudad Juárez area. If the local gang leader knew they were making a profit, he would demand his share – thus the name, Guerilla Prayer Flags.

I asked Sara if I could help in some way. She suggested that I could help sell the prayer flags, and I was welcome to meet the women. "I think they would just like to have someone from the U.S. come visit them and listen to their stories."

A few weeks later, I followed Sara over the border, and eventually met Inéz, Cuca, Minerva, Dr. Mendoza, Linabel, Elvia, and their friends. Most of the women have worked in the factories. They have crossed into the United States with the required documents and without. Some have children with disabilities. And all are involved in formal and informal support structures.

PRIVILEGE DISTORTIONS

Books are written by those who have the wealth, education, and leisure to write their interpretation of a story. Thus, for most of history we have been dependent on interpretations from the privileged lens. I have those White privileges, plus the advantage of command of a powerful, dominant language. However, I have learned that those privileges also develop a distorted, ignorant, sometimes blinded view of the world.

The women I met in this study have fewer privileges. Their stories help us understand why. They welcomed me into their homes and gave me open permission to use their stories. I did pay them a little for sharing their valuable time with the promise that, if a publication came from the stories, the profit would be shared with the women's support centers described in this book.

Those months of interviews and observations provide only a slice of their worlds. Some of the details and descriptions came from my interpretation of their words through a U.S. lens and my less-than-perfect understanding of their Mexican culture and Spanish language. Yet, I worked hard to minimize the distortion. To maintain fidelity to the women's stories, I recorded and typed my translations as accurately as possible. I took rough translations back to the women. They offered slight modifications if any. Each woman and representative of the organizations gave written approval to use their stories as they are organized and presented here. Some women requested I use a pseudonym.

The stories of my tossing candy to the children and bringing strappy high heels to Anapra illustrate my cultural distortion. My focus improved as I walked and talked with women who were holding up a shaky sky. Their stories ache to be projected to a wider audience – to expand understanding of how a woman's persistent grit can grow beauty in a harsh world.

~ 2 ~

INÉZ

"For Christmas we had a *tamalada* for all the family and friends and neighbors. I don't know how many people were here – oh, more than a hundred. We bought a whole pig from the butcher. And we made thirty kilos [66 pounds] of tamales! It was a huge mess and there were people everywhere. That was my happiest day. Now I am at peace."

Inéz wears her light brown hair in a short, sassy cut that highlights her golden complexion and contrasts with her gentle manner. We met in her home where a small television, a portable air conditioner, couches, and shelves with books and family photos fill the main living area. The walls are covered with family-generated art – from a three-year-old's scribble-coloring of a valentine to the lacquered wooden plaque expressing love for Jesus, made by her oldest son while he was in prison. He is home now and safe with his family after enduring a year in a Mexican jail for one night's reckless behavior.

The workshop where the women make the Guerilla Prayer Flags is tucked in one corner of Inéz's land. She owns this lot in Anapra, about a quarter acre in size. She lives in the main house with her daughter, Elvia, who is attending the university in Ciudad Juárez studying social work, and her youngest child, Adam, who is in high school. A rock and wire fence defines this plot which includes her house and three smaller houses: one for her daughter, Rita, and her family; one for her son, Andres, and his family; and one for her son, Gabriel, and his family. Inéz's younger sister, Lina, and her family live a few blocks away. All her neighbors are close friends. She tells me that they feel safe now as they share resources and watch out for each other.

I visited several times from 2017 through 2020. On my first visit, Inéz showed me her house and her land. Her official family includes her children, several grand-children, nieces, and nephews. Her community family was even larger.

MONDAY MARKET

Every Monday, Inéz, her older daughter, Rita, and her daughter-in-law go to the market in downtown Ciudad Juárez. They meet at Inez's house. The produce is much cheaper at the market than at the S-Mart, the only grocery store (similar to a Wal-Mart) in Anapra.

That morning, Rita, with four-year-old Josue and two-year-old David, came into the house. Rita dresses very stylish with a little funk – short, curly black hair and large framed glasses, tight pants, and Converse tennis shoes. When they entered, the little boys ran to their grand-mother. Inéz relished the love. Rita greeted me and went down the hall to get the rolling cart and plastic tubs to carry the groceries. Daughter-in-law Ana met us outside at Inéz's 2000 van.

They gave me the good seat up front beside Inéz; the others sat on benches in the back. We parked downtown in a fenced lot and paid the attendant his fee. The girls attached the two large plastic tubs onto a handcart using bungee cords. Rita hiked the baby on her hip, Josue held onto his grandmother's hand, and we walked a few blocks to the huge market.

This market is a hub of pedestrian streets bustling with shoppers and vendors and lined with produce: a vast assortment of vegetables, live chickens, ready-for-the-pot chickens plucked and hanging on hooks, boxes filled with the wonders of Mexican fruit, dried beans and rice, honey, eggs, and stalls selling cooked food. Bent-over men lugged huge loads of produce on their backs from a truck parked down the street to the designated booth or shop. Booths for clothing, candy, and inexpensive toys were located on the outer edges of the market.

Inéz and her girls walked to specific locations where they waited in line with the other savvy shoppers to get the very best prices. Later we all huddled in a small space between a storefront and a booth; Inéz and I were holding tight to the little ones while the girls packed the produce most carefully in the plastic tubs.

Last stop was to purchase eggs to feed the families for the week. The vendor sold them on open slats holding thirty-six eggs. The girls purchased four slats and carefully secured them on top of the plastic tubs as we started our trip back to the van. We were all carrying plastic bags of produce, and Rita was trying to manage pulling the cart, carrying her bag, and holding the baby. We lost some eggs. The young mothers giggled to buffer a hopeless situation.

When we got to the parking lot, Inéz said she needed

to walk to the bank building to pay her phone bill. Josue and I went with her; Rita and Ana stayed at the van with the baby to load the produce. We stood in line for a few minutes with other customers who had to pay in-person every month. As we were walking out of the building, Josue convinced his grandmother to stop at the street vendor's table where there was a display of toys – in particular, a set of yellow plastic tools. Inéz could not say no, but she warned him not to open the package until they got home. He agreed and he held his new toy carefully all the way home. He chatted continually; he had a lot to tell his grandmother about this new toy.

Before we left, Inéz led us around the block for our treat from the *paleta* vendor selling world famous Mexican popsicles – flavors such as mango, pecan, coconut, caramel cream, rich vanilla, and Mexican chocolate.

THE LITTLE MECHANIC

As soon as we got back to Inéz's house, the girls unpacked and divided the produce. Inéz got a knife and helped Josue open the wrap over his plastic tools. The skinny little scamp is never still, and now he was jumping with excitement. I sat on the couch and observed the activity. Josue interpreted my sitting still as an invitation to play with him. His voice is high-pitched, and he speaks rapidly and continually. Although I could not understand much of his chatter, he made it clear what he wanted.

He handed me his tools, explaining each one carefully and telling me his name for each: hammer, wrench, pliers, and screwdriver. Then he left me to guard them while he went into Inéz's hallway where he dragged out a folding aluminum lounge chair, the kind with rubber tubing wrapped around the frame. He set the chair on the floor in front of me and spread out the head and foot sections so that it was a flat bed.

He slid underneath the lounge chair, stuck his hand out at my leg, and said, "*martillo.*" I handed him the hammer. He used it a little while to change the oil or repair the engine underneath the lounge chair. Then he handed the little hammer back to me and said something which I guessed was pliers. I was right and he fixed another part of his "car," chattering away as he twisted his toy tools and hammered on the aluminum frame.

I caught Inéz's eye and she smiled a grandmother smile. I kept assisting the smart little mechanic while Inéz cut up a cantaloupe, blended it in the blender, and added ice water and sugar to make *agua melon.* The beans that had been simmering all morning were smashed into *frijoles.* She tore the meat off a roasted chicken and set it out by the beans with a stack of fresh tortillas wrapped in a moist cloth.

Guadalupe, Rita, Ana, Adam, and several little children streamed in and out, each filling a plate with food and a glass with *agua melon.* There was not room for everyone to eat together, so some stood at the kitchen counter or balanced plates in their laps as they sat in the living room. No one needed silverware. Tortillas are a tasty way to transport food.

When Josue gave me a break, I joined the women standing around the counter. Guadalupe, an attractive woman with her hair in a bun, had been working in the prayer-flag workshop behind the house, dyeing the cloth squares and hanging them on the drying racks. Her face was still glistening from the heat.

As she ate, she told me about her daughter, Montserrat, named after a black Madonna and child in a cathedral in Catalonia. Montserrat, at that time ten years old, had cerebral spastic palsy and was confined to a special wheelchair. She was having therapy at the clinic that morning. "She is my world, my special gift from God. That is why I named her after the Virgin."

I asked Guadalupe if she had any help caring for Montserrat. "No. In the United States the government helps special children a lot. Here there is no help. Well, not in the schools. The Sisters at Santo Niño help so much. She can do things because they stimulate her brain. They do miracles with her. I live with my mother, but it is upstairs. I carry her up and down the stairs.

"I did have a husband, but when she was born, I had to care for the baby all the time. I couldn't care for him, so he left. Men don't stick around if you have a special needs child." The other women nodded. Lupe looked at the clock, "Oh! I have to go pick her up now." Then she gave everyone in the room a hug with an air kiss near the cheek, the traditional warm Mexican farewell, and rushed out the door.

Inéz had cleaned up the lunch mess while Guadalupe was telling her story.

The other women and children returned to their own houses. Inéz's youngest child, fourteen-year-old Adam, settled on the living room couch to watch one of the Ninja Turtle movies. Inéz nudged him into action, "Fill the water jars before you watch tele." He slugged to his feet, got the two-gallon plastic containers, went outside to the large water storage tank, and returned with the drinking water.

"We can talk in my office," she said as she led me down the hallway. I followed her past the bathroom and two small rooms for Elvia and Adam. She stopped. "Right there, where the bathroom is, that is where my little house started – the first room where I made a store and was selling candy."

We entered her office. She moved the folding massage table up against the shelves and pulled out her desk chair for me to sit. "I give massage therapy. But sometimes they come in saying, 'My shoulder hurts.' So I give the massage, and then I say to them, 'Something more than your shoulder hurts. Tell me more about it.' So, I also give talk therapy." She opened a window so we had a breeze and then sat on the small couch.

TWO HUGS A YEAR

"Do you know my first memory as a little girl? Not playing or being happy. No, my first memory was my older brother on top of me on the bed having sex with me. I was just three years old.

"When I was six years old, I told my mother what he was doing. She said, 'Shhh, Inéz! You are telling a lie.' That killed something inside me. I was afraid to talk, so I quit talking. I thought that my words were lies; telling lies was bad. I was the cause of the bad things. It was my fault, and no one cared.

"We lived in the area near the Santa Fe Bridge in downtown Juárez. My mother was working from eight in the morning to eight at night as a maid for a rich family in

Juárez. My mother had three girls and three boys, each three years apart. We all had different fathers. None of us knew our fathers. We were left alone all day. My brother was abusing all of us.

"He made me go begging in El Paso. I remember he would kick me and pull my arm. He screamed at me to quit wiggling so he could smear chocolate on my face, to look dirty and poor, you know. He pulled my hair up in a messy ponytail and twisted it in a rubber band. Oh, that hurt! Then he dragged me from our house to the river, just a few blocks. There was no water in the river and no fence like they have now.

"We went to the main plaza in the center of El Paso where they had the alligators in the fountain [an iconic attraction in El Paso's central plaza]. Then he gave me a cup and pushed me out to go begging from the people. He would go sit in the shade. Here I am, going up to people and saying, '*Por favor, ayudame.*' I guess I looked so pathetic that they did give me money. I had to give it to my brother, and he kept all the money.

"I have a memory of a nice lady who sold trinkets in a small store. My mother took me and my sister to the lady's store one day. The lady asked my mother if she could keep me, raise me as her own child. My heart was full of hope; maybe I would be in a home where I was protected, safe. Mother told her no and we left.

"My mother gave us hugs, but only two times a year. One was our birthday and the other was Christmas. No, no," she corrected herself, "she didn't hug on Christmas. It was New Year's Day. Two hugs a year. Not a long hug. Just a short one.

"I tried to win Mama's love. I made her these house

shoes and wrapped them up for her. After she opened them, she went next door and gave them to the neighbor. And she took me with her to watch.

"I did the laundry. Folded the clothes so neat and put them on the shelves. I cleaned the house every day. When I was older, I prepared food – chicken pies, tamales, red chile. Then she sold the food at the maquiladoras. Never any thank you. I felt empty.

"By the time I was eight years old, I was doing most of the cooking, all of the cleaning and the laundry. And I was caring for Lina, who was five, and another baby, little, maybe two years. Our mother just went to work and came home and slept. She did some cooking on her day off. Then, our mom invited three little nieces and nephews to come live with us. I had to care for all of them!

"When I was sixteen years old, my mother beat me because I was cutting hair for some people, and I was making money. She kicked me out. I lived on the street, sometimes with friends, trying to go to school. I found a job at a maquiladora. I had no place to stay. I was so tired. Sometimes I could stay with a friend. Sometimes I stayed all night at the café downtown that is open twenty-four hours. I would study and then the waitress would wake me up. I had to keep ordering coffee.

"That is why I married the first man, Felipe. I was his secretary at the maquiladora. My life decisions were made of sheer desperation. All three husbands were my only option out of desperation."

LOVE OUT OF DESPERATION

By age thirteen, Inez's little sister Lina was old enough to take over the housework and care for the five younger children. Inéz was not so valuable to her mother anymore, so she was on her own. That is when she married Felipe "out of desperation."

"Felipe had the idea that if we both worked at the maquiladora and took extra shifts, we could make a little booth to sell hamburgers outside the maquiladora at the shift changes. There are thousands of hungry employees getting off work three times every day. We could live at his brother's house.

"I said okay, but I want to go back to school. He said that is why we would make the hamburger booth. We will have more time and more money. Then we could both go to school. Well, I needed a home. If Felipe's dreams came true, I would get to finish school. So, I accepted.

"We lived in a small room in the house with his brother's family. We both worked very hard and saved every penny. I bought a small grill and experimented with various hamburgers until we found the right one. We grilled the meat over a hot flame until it had a crust, then we put cheese, avocado, ham, bacon, lettuce, tomato, pickles, mustard, mayonnaise, and catsup with chilies on the side. We bought a tent, a work surface, two grills, and a few chairs and set up outside of the biggest factories. And we were still working in the maquiladora.

"That is when they gave me this land. Then Anapra was just a few buildings. They wanted more workers to live near the factories. And they sent buses here so you could get to your shift on time.

"They invited some people who worked in the factories to a meeting. We could select a plot of land. I was one of the last, so my land was the worst one. A big rainstorm had washed an arroyo right through it. We couldn't live there at first. Later I built a fence, by myself, rock by rock, and I had to fill in the arroyo. I dug the septic tank by myself. This land has saved me, but it caused me much trouble.

"Of course, now they want me to pay a fee, taxes, to the city because the land is much more valuable. They are putting in more and more factories near here. I think they might want to take the land away because it is more valuable.

"Well, Felipe and I were living in a little house in Juárez then. Felipe worked hard. He was a gentle man. He had a good economic sense, and by the third year of marriage, we had expanded to our own small restaurant in a building in downtown Juárez with eight tables and six employees. The hamburgers became famous and the profits were good. We lived well. Then I got pregnant.

"It was the most stable time to have a child, but my body rejected the baby. I was sick all the time until Gabriel was born.

"Then, you know what happened? One night, Felipe pulled out a bag of cocaine and asked me to try it. I panicked! My brother used drugs and I knew what life would be like with drugs. No, never with my husband. I got my clothes and Gabriel and ran to my mother's house. Felipe came looking for me and the baby. He was friends with the police, judge, other officials. I was terrified that he would hurt me and take the baby."

CROSSING TO THE UNITED STATES

"To get away from him, I crossed to the north with another man, my Canadian. First, we went to Mexicali. The Canadian had relatives in California, and my sister, Rosario, lived in San Diego. The Canadian crossed first and took little Gabriel to my sister. I was waiting in Mexicali until I could pay the *coyote* to take me across. I had to wait many months until the *coyote* was ready, and I gave him five hundred dollars. We crossed the hot desert, walking. It took weeks. Horrible! But we made it and went to a tiny apartment – just one room for all sixteen of us. We were so hot and hungry. We stayed three days there.

"Finally, my Canadian found me, and we got Gabriel and went to San Francisco. We were just selling things on the street, living under a bridge. I found a women's shelter for me and Gabriel. And I was pregnant with Andres. I stayed there for several months. It was comfortable – food, a bed, and classes in English, with childcare, and training in cosmetology. But I was always lonely and cold. The shelter was temporary, you could only stay a few months.

"One day when my Canadian was under the bridge, *La Migra* [immigration enforcement officials] got him and he was deported to Canada. Also, I found out that he had been using drugs. Lina and my mother were living on my land in a trailer. [Inéz took me to the window and pointed to the travel trailer.] See, that is the trailer. It is still there – so small and so old.

"Lina called me and told me that Felipe had a new wife and baby. It should be safe if I wanted to come home. I went to some churches in San Francisco, begging for help, and they gave me enough money to go back to Juárez.

Finally, I was home. No money, no job, no house. But I was home. Mother let us sleep in the tiny trailer – my mother, Lina and Lina's baby, and me and my two little boys. HA!"

A HOME OF HER OWN

Inéz worked her land. She started picking up rocks and stacking them to make a fence. She filled in the large arroyo with tires, rocks, old pieces of wood, anything to fill that hole. The water that had washed out the arroyo came from the uphill neighbor's land during rainstorms. She had to work hard to convince him to fill in his part of the arroyo.

She gathered up old packing pallets, old tires, leftover plywood and created a small shed at the street edge of her property. It was raw – no floor other than the sand, one electric light bulb drawing off of a cable that a neighbor pirated from the city's electric line several blocks away, and a barrel out front for water if she could pay seventy cents when the water truck drove by each week.

Then she asked her mother to lend her $50.00. It was not easy to pry the money from that woman, but eventually Inéz had $50.00. She left little Gabriel and Andres with her mother, the only time she would leave them.

She walked the few miles to the large market in the center of Juárez. She purchased all the candy that $50.00 would buy, lugged it home, set up a shelf in the front of her little shed, and started selling candy and haircuts. She doubled her money in four days, reinvested the profits in candy, and kept the store open from seven in the morning until nine each night, or as long as there were customers.

Within a few weeks, she had enough profit to pay someone to pour a concrete porch for her store and the first room of her little house. She had income and she could watch over and care for the babies, and, in between customers, dig a septic tank and continue working on her rock fence. This was home. But peace was far in the distance.

RAMIRO AND ADAM

"The next phase was very difficult. My little store was sufficient for me and the children. One day, my younger brother came to live with me. He had been deported from El Paso. He came with his wife and two little sons. They got work in the maquiladoras, so I had to care for four children, fix all the food, and run the store. I couldn't say no to them. But it was awful, and I was more than a year living like a slave. No time for me or my children. It was killing me.

"So, I ran to another man. Someone to take me away so I could be in peace. For two years, this man had been asking me and asking me to go with him. He always came by the store. That was Ramiro. We were together many years. At that time, I called it love, but it was sheer necessity.

"I married Ramiro and moved to his house. My brother and his wife took over the little store. Ramiro was a worker in construction. He was responsible. I was calm now with my kids. For me it was okay. But he was very stingy. He was never satisfied.

"After a few months, my brother and his family left. Ramiro came here, to my land, with me. He didn't want me to work in my store, didn't want me to leave the house. He wanted his food ready on time. He didn't want me to have friends. He was *muy machistoso*. By now, I had also had Rita and then Elvia.

"My children were in school, except little Elvia. A depression overcame me. So, with little Elvia I went to the counseling center, Las Hormigas, to the therapy. I kept that hidden – he never knew – for many years. This was a calm time. I got the therapy. I was learning and healing. Elvia got to go to the school at Las Hormigas. Things were getting better *poco a poco*.

"He developed liver cancer. He drank a lot, but he was not an aggressive drunk. He had a pension that we lived on, about one hundred fifty dollars per month. The money lasted only a few years. He was too sick to work. I began working a lot, mostly cleaning hospitals. Even his last year, I was still working.

She stopped talking. Large tears fell from her eyes. We paused until she got her voice back. "Then I was pregnant with Adam. He still wanted sex even when he was so sick. I did not want it; he was dying. It was a rape; he forced me. And I got pregnant. I had to take care of everything and a bad pregnancy. I just couldn't manage.

"When I went into labor, it was the hardest time of my life. Adam just wouldn't come out. His head was crowning and stuck there. It was so painful it paralyzed me. His head was stuck! There were doctors, but they didn't know how to manage this. The pain was horrible, horrible. The worst pain I ever felt. Finally, after, oh, many hours, a new nurse came in. She got on top of me and pushed my stomach from the top. Just kept pushing until he finally came out. Adam suffers from that also. All the pain and trouble are still with him.

"After the birth, I had a high temperature. I couldn't get out of bed. Every part of my body was burning, and I couldn't even lift a finger. Mom, sister, never came to help me. A friend came to help a little. I didn't have money. I didn't have my store. I couldn't work. We went days with no food for the kids. I had volunteered in the church for years, but the priest didn't come help me. This went on for two years. And I found out that Ramiro had sexually abused little Elvia. It was just horrible. Why did no one come to help me? Adam suffered all this with me. It affected him. He is still troubled. [She paused, sobbing.]

"Ramiro was very sick. I got through it because of my kids. When there was no more food and medicine, I got up and did what I could with the baby in my arm and all that pain. One priest had this program – once a week he had food free for any person. He gave me chicken, eggs, potatoes, carrots. Father Jim, he brought food for us. The Baptists gave free burritos to the kids before school. My kids ate the Baptist burritos. Without that, they would have starved some days.

She was still crying. I held her hand. "We can stop here. You need a break. Those were dark times," I told her.

"Yes, but you come back. I want to tell you how I got through it all...how we fought to get our land, water, schools, jobs. We fought for all of those things."

WE NEED LAND AND WATER. IF NOT, WE CROSS TO EL NORTE.

Our next visit was all business. She wanted to tell me the rest of her story.

"We need land and water. If we have that, we can live here in our home. If not, we try to cross to El Norte. But we had to fight for our water. Some years, depending on the politicians in charge, they sent big trucks with water, *las pipas*, to our house, not for drinking, but water for cleaning. Sometimes it was free, but now we pay for it. It is not too much. If we are home, they will fill our barrels or tanks with water. We had to buy all our drinking water and carry it into our houses. Then about fifteen years ago, they put in a water line from the city water to the houses, but it comes from the aquifer which is too salty. If you drink it, you will get sick. And it is bad for the kids.

"Later the city put in one line for clean water, and you can get that clean water, two gallons of water per person per day. You can see people with their wagons and carts carrying the water. You can only get it in the morning three days per week at the three water centers they have in Anapra.

"But get this, when we first moved here, maybe twenty years ago, one of the *politicos* campaigned saying they would not give any water to Anapra! Can you believe it? *No agua por Anapra!* That was his campaign! No city truck came to our houses. You could pay for the private water truck to deliver the water. There was just one company. That was not enough for us. Some old people and children were dying.

"One day, we saw one of the city *pipa* trucks, and I

joined the girls and our neighbors and kids. We climbed on the truck and we would not get down. That *pipa* went to our neighborhood and gave all of us all free water. He never came back. But the newspaper saw it, and we came out in the newspaper.

"Then we all got together a big protest march, five hundred of us, carrying empty buckets, dirty clothes, rub boards, and we marched from here to the mayor's office [about five miles]. The TV stations were there. The next day we had *pipas* delivering water to us for free." She nodded with a smile.

FIGHTING FOR THE SCHOOL IN THE SAND

"My kids started elementary school at Jaime Torres Bodet.[2]

I had to fight for a school too. The school was just cardboard shacks in the sand. We fought hard to get fences, electricity, buildings. We invited the news reporters to come see the school, and we were fighting all the time for those things. We tried letters and phone calls, but that didn't do anything. We did a lot of protests.

"At the kindergarten they didn't have a fence, and the cows came onto the children's playground. So, we kidnapped the teachers and had protests outside the school. We invited the press to come to the protests. Channel Sixteen News was there. We had signs. We locked the teachers in one of the big rooms until the school agreed to resolve the problem.

---

[2] That is the same school my UTEP students collaborated with.

"The chiefs of public education came, and in the end, they made new rooms for the school and built fences. Of course, we asked the teachers if we could kidnap them. They all said yes, and they had their books and food and water in the room. One teacher wanted to get a job as a leader, so she didn't want to be kidnapped. That was fine. We let her go."

WHO CAN HURT ME NOW?

"It took me many years to overcome the lack of love and the abuses. I went to therapy for sixteen years." Her eyes were downcast as she nodded to some memory in her thoughts. "Las Hormigas. They had projects to help women who have been abused. Now, I am able to forgive my mother and my brother. In one of the therapy sessions, they asked, 'Who can hurt me the most, the men who abused me, or me – if I continue to hold onto the hurt.' Who really can hurt me?" She looked up and pointed to her chest. "ME! I have that power to hurt or protect myself.

"How I found out about Las Hormigas? Well, they sent people into communities to tell about the projects for personal development for Anapra women. They taught us: Who is in charge of you? Is it yourself? Is it your abusive brother? Is it your unloving mother? You have the power to say who is in charge.

"I learned that I didn't need to keep begging for my mother's love because she did not have any to give me. I changed a lot after I realized that. I knew it was me who allowed them to keep hurting me. I was more open without all that built-up hurt. The counseling gave me self-empowerment, courage, love, power. I finally accepted that it was not my fault. I learned that the abuse will always be a part of me, but it is not guiding me. It is more of a step to take me higher.

"In my therapy I realized that I did learn important things from my mother. I learned how *not* to live and how *not* to treat children. I am not going to allow that for my children or other children.

"One good thing; because of my abuse, I can see it in other women. There was a little girl, maybe four years old, walking down my street. Instantly I could see that she was being abused. I told the mother, 'Please, watch her carefully. Investigate.' They did and found that a ten-year-old boy had been touching her. Sadly, we can only prevent it by watching and investigating. We really can't accuse abusers or punish them.

"Now, I am at peace. I have happiness inside of me. I don't really know how I did it. There is just something inside of me. I work at the Clinic. I teach Tai Chi to the mothers at Santa Niño. I do massage therapy. I manage the prayer flags. I learned to accept my love for myself so that I can love others."

SMALL BUSINESS PROJECTS

"When Ramiro got sick, I had to work. Three children were in school, so we had more expenses. Some of my friends from Las Hormigas and my neighbors, about ten of us, tried different projects. First, we worked sewing clothes, adding beads, repair, alterations. But we were not making any profit. They just weren't buying those clothes. Then we made little bags. Those didn't sell well either.

"Then, in 2003, we had the idea to take people to the S-Mart to get groceries. A taxi is very expensive. We got a grant from Las Hormigas to buy a used van, and we women took turns driving our route. It was just for some of the houses far from the store, and we charged less than a dollar. We had Uber before there was Uber! We won a prize for this idea – Brave Women Prize – and we went to Mexico City to get the prize.

"Well, there is a bus system here in Anapra, and they have a route which goes from one end of the main street to the other, back and forth. It was just one bus, and it doesn't help you get your groceries back to your house. We were not using their route. But the bus system fought with us. It was all men. And we were women.

"One day, I was driving the van and two big buses surrounded my van. They pulled my hair, trying to drag me out of the van; they said they would kill me. Some of the people at S-Mart came and started yelling at the drivers and helped me get away from them. But their threat was real, so we quit driving our van.

"Next, we had the idea to sell food out of the van. I sold hamburgers there for a while. But it was hard with my kids. We tried to make a little restaurant, but the *narco* bosses found out and wanted big fees for our business. We needed something we could do that would be hidden where they couldn't see us making our money. And something we could do while we care for our children with special needs. We all have special children. So many troubles here in Anapra with the food, the poisons in the air, soil, water. And the poor medical care, like the doctor who didn't know how to help me with Adam when he was born.

"After we made those bags we tried to sell, Lina said, 'Why not flags?' We wanted something very organic. First, we made them by recycling old white tee shirts. Lina sewed. I painted and inked them. Guadalupe put the print on. Others cut cloth, then put them on a string. Packed them in the bags. It is a long process. They look like Tibetan prayer flags.

"We decided to call them Guerilla Prayer Flags because we made them in secret. Selling was hard. We went to various places in El Paso like Whole Foods. And in Las Cruces, events where we could have a table. Sara sold them on the farmers market. We went to churches and with the Maya weaving group. Here and there. Sara helps so much because she sells them at places over the border, like the *Dia de los Muertos* in Mesilla.

"Here in Juárez nobody buys them. They sell for fifteen dollars, which is three days' salary at a maquiladora. We put them on Etsy. Now we are Guadalupe, Lina, Cuca, Sandra, Rita, and me. Now it is sustainable. The business pays a little to each of us.

"To me now, the purpose of making these is for the women to practice mindfulness. I tell them that this is their love they are giving to the world, and anyone in the world can see the flag and can tell if they put their love into it. And we have pictures of a wedding in Chile decorated with prayer flags, even a picture of prayer flags going with the climbers up Mt. Everest! So, we want good quality.

"Primarily, I want the women to practice mindfulness. If they are not at peace, the love will not show in their flags. The dye [process] is slow and deliberate, and it must be perfect. The edges must be carefully done. Lina needs to focus her mind on this project of love and the troubles in her life are outside of her while she is sewing the flags. When Sandra irons the flags, she is developing her inner peace as she thinks of the flag going out into the world. It is really a pretext to their therapy. Look deep inside yourself. You can be free even if you live in a jail. Or you can be in jail in your spirit even if you are free."

TO LIVE, NOT JUST SURVIVE

"Shortly after Ramiro died, I was driving the van for Santo Niño Clinic. I went to a house and saw the worst thing ever. The mother was insane. She had babies and trash all over. She had a daughter who was a wild animal. She was locked in a small room with nothing, naked, raging. That was Miriam.

"The nuns from the clinic went to that house. I was getting a little better and able to drive the van for the nuns. They paid me a little money. They brought Miriam to the clinic. She was crazy wild, hitting and biting all the people. But not the little children. Something in her told her to be gentle with the little ones.

"I would start to interact with her so gently. She responded to me. I could keep her calm. I had learned how to live with peace inside of myself despite abuse. I was helping her find some peace. She was still wild, but the therapy was working. I began to really love that child. I was at my lowest point in life, and this wild child needed the little that I had left to give. That turned into love.

"I had been just helping at the clinic, driving and

sweeping. But the nuns saw how I worked with Miriam, and they started training me in massage therapy and the other therapies. They did not want Miriam to go back to her mother's house.

"The Sisters asked me if Miriam could live with me. Lina took her half time, and I took her half time. She stayed with us three years. Soon she was using the bathroom, playing nicely with my children, and she would laugh. She could still be violent. The doctor gave her some calming medicine and making those doses work the best was also part of learning how to work with her.

"Miriam was such a part of our family. We loved her for three years. But she was officially under state care. And, since she was eighteen, an adult, and we were not part of her blood family, they took her away. We never knew what happened to her.

"By now, I was one of the therapists at the clinic. I had that talent. After this, I was able to *vivir más que solo sobrevivir* – to live, not just survive.

"God is not a set of rules or the words of the Pope. God is much bigger. Love is much bigger. And now, life has given me so much to share."

WATER IN ANAPRA

Water – its demand, its scarcity, its salinity, its political and economic control, and its danger in a summer storm as it carves canyons in the streets – water dominates the life in Anapra. Inéz talked about chasing the water trucks in Anapra and fighting the city to provide water to this area of Juárez. She won that battle. She made me taste the salty water that came from her tap and took me to the small water utility station where we picked up two five-gallon jugs, her weekly allocation of free drinking water.

In my visits to the community in the early 2000s, there were no water lines. All water came from the big tank trucks. Some years, it was delivered free. Other years, the citizens had to pay for the service. Every home had a container of some kind out in front of the house, easily accessed by the hose from the water truck. The cleanliness of those containers was questionable. I drove through puddles in the sandy streets where wastewater flowed.

At the time of this writing, most homes are connected to the city wastewater pipes or septic tanks. I do not see sewer water in the streets now. Water for washing (not drinking) is available to most of the residents of Anapra via water lines into their homes or a nearby outdoor spigot. That water comes from an aquifer that is nearing depletion. Things have improved, but abundant, clean water in Anapra has always been and will remain a serious problem.

~ 3 ~

PROYECTO SANTO NIÑO

LIFE TEACHES US

In the Catholic faith, *Santo Niño de Atocha* is a representation of Jesus as a child, and it is said he traveled throughout Mexican rural areas performing miracles and healing sick children.

A community center dedicated to children's health, called *Proyecto Santo Niño*, is located a few blocks from Inéz's house, up the sandy street towards the southern edge of Anapra. A concrete ramp with railings leads to the front door of the bright blue building with a large painting of the Virgin of Guadalupe on the outside wall.

A highly respected priest from the Columbian Order who served in Anapra used to live in the building, and, when he left, he gave it to a group of nuns from the Sisters of Charity, an order in Cincinnati; but this group of Sisters relocated to live in southern New Mexico very near the Mexican border. They cross over three or four times per week to manage *Proyecto Santo Niño*.

The main room in the building is an open activity center, approximately fifteen by twenty-five feet, with a kitchen in the back corner. The back door, near the kitchen, leads to an enclosed covered patio with a children's play fort, a climbing wall, stairs, and a slide. The bottom of the slide rests in a large sandbox. Storage and restrooms are near the entrance. On the west side is a large room with six massage-style tables and three smaller rooms set up for tutoring sessions.

My first visit was in the summer of 2019. Three nuns from the Sisters of Charity and several of the mothers were working with children. Most of the children had visible and severe disabilities. Everyone was greeted warmly with the air kiss on the cheek and much hugging and fussing over the little ones.

Three mothers were preparing snacks and lunch. Three other mothers were going through a bag of used clothing and distributing items that would fit the children. They called out, *"Lupe, this blouse might fit Monserrat,"* or *"Oh, Ella, look at these cute sweatpants for Carlos."* Ella put the new sweatpants on Carlos – an eight-year-old with no muscle control. As she held him up, the other mothers cooed over how cute he was in his new pants. He smiled a giant slobbery smile.

Gloria, an elderly woman leaning on a cane, entered the room. I sat at a table beside Chuy, a very large boy, about twelve years old, with Down syndrome. I offered a fist bump, and he responded with a gentle bump and a big smile. Eventually there were approximately twenty children and fifteen women. Three teenage boys were tossing a ball in the activity room. Sister Carol sat down beside me, introduced herself, and explained much of what I was witnessing.

The organization began in 2003 as a clinic to provide much needed health care in this remote area of Juárez. However, it changed over the years as the needs in the community became more evident. Carol pointed to the woman with a cane who had been their first client at the original clinic when she came to them pregnant with no family or money. She has been coming regularly to the center ever since, and the care she receives from the Sisters has kept her and her special needs child alive.

When Reyna, a seven-year-old with Down syndrome in a sparkly pink dress, came in with her mother, she climbed up in Carol's lap to get the hugs that came with that lap. Her mother, after hugs and air kisses with the Sisters and her friends, got busy preparing the materials for the children's activities about to take place in the large activity center. Carol told me Reyna's mother was fifteen and an orphan living on the streets when she came to the clinic, pregnant with Reyna. Now Reyna calls Sister Carol *Abuelita* (grandmother), and her mother is one of the paid teachers at the center.

After most had gathered, soft music started playing. Inéz stood in the middle of the activity room and the children and mothers began to join her in a circle. Inéz never said a word, it all just happened. It took about fifteen minutes to get everyone in the circle and focused. Inéz started Tai Chi motions. Mothers, nuns, and the children who were able followed the movements' sway in harmony. Tai Chi and sometimes CBD oil are helpful in calming the attention deficit hyperactivity disorder which most of the children are dealing with.

After the Tai Chi session, the younger children stayed in the activity center. Sister Romina and Rita led these children in activities and songs for early literacy development. They varied group activities with structured play using materials like modeling clay, puzzles, coloring books, stencils, and building logs. When Rita sat on the carpet with a book, most of the children left their table activities and joined her. Chuy's mother was helping in the preschool classroom.

The children with more severe special needs, and Gloria with her cane, were assisted to the therapy room where they took turns on the therapy tables. Carol and Inéz led the sessions using a form of Reiki massage and movement to stimulate neural pathways. Two other mothers were also doing the therapy with Carol and Inéz's guidance. Carol told me that this therapy approach focuses on movement to develop brain plasticity.

Other children went into the classrooms where Sister Andrea and one of the mothers helped them with more advanced learning activities. Carol explained, "The children who were able to go to public school still needed much academic support, so we started the school here three years ago. The two mothers who are now our teachers are great. One of our Sisters is a master teacher. She trains the mothers and manages the curriculum. We are paying about nine women a little each week. There are fifteen children officially in the school, but their brothers and sisters come also. We are constantly learning with the families.

"After a few years with our clinic, we saw that the need here was tremendous. We were not just a clinic anymore, but a place to help these many families and their children with special needs. I hit a plateau of what I could do to help with these physical and learning disabilities. Then I saw a TED talk on a method of neural movement. I found the program and studied with them for four years. We found that using this method with these kids was life-giving.

"We do what presents itself, following the wisdom of the founder of our order, Sister Blandina. The clinic presented itself when the community had no clinic. When the new clinic was built in Anapra, we changed to focus on the new needs – to this [she swept her hand across the room] – helping families of children with disabilities.

"The massage therapy presented itself. The school presented itself. Training the mothers presented itself. As you get to know people and their stories, the need will present itself. The therapy we were giving was too much for us to manage. So, we trained Inéz and other mothers. Inéz was a widow with five children when we started. She helped us by driving the van to pick up families. She and the other mothers were eager to learn. Inéz had the touch to do the Reiki. She uses the hand positions that can draw up the person's own energy, their own healing. But we also do large muscle movement for neural development."

The Santo Niño project illustrates the difference between charity – a top-down handout – and altruism – a horizontal relationship between the gift and the recipient, mutual benefit flowing both ways.

THE COMMUNAL HEART

"Here, there is a communal heart. When you get the attitude that you are going to fix or change something, it will not work. I come here with great joy. I love seeing these miracles with the people. Wherever the project goes, we will do it together. I cannot say I am helping them. We are just with them. Watching the young mothers teaching the children just gets into my heart."

Rita interrupted Inéz as she was doing massage. "Look, Mamá, Josue just wrote his name. See! He can write!"

Sister Carol told me Rita was a great teacher. They dreamed that she could go to a university to get her degree. And, when I visited a few months later, Rita told me that she was indeed going to the University Cultural in Juárez every Saturday. Her classes are history, pedagogy, and psychology. She has a lot of homework, but she is loving it. "I am so happy now. I teach craft classes in my house, and it helps me pay for my school."

I visited again in late February. It was a cold day, but the building was cozy with butane heaters. I watched the learning activities again. The learning materials are high quality and keep the children's attention. The building was being upgraded and renovated, so activities were happening in every corner.

I chatted with one of the mothers, Yoli, who was helping Jesus with tactile function. Jesus has cerebral paralysis and other conditions. He was in a wheelchair, and I did not see any movement indicating attention to his surroundings. He seemed calm with Yoli holding his hand and running dry rice, beans, and pasta over his fingers. His mother sat down beside us. She said he has been coming here since he was a baby, nine years ago. When he was younger, he had severe convulsions, and the doctors said he would not live but a few months. "Santo Niño has helped him so much and now he sleeps through the night and has few convulsions. *Un milagro*!" [A miracle]. Every mother was busy helping some child.

Isidra and her team of three volunteers had lunch ready around noon. I was invited to join them – spicy meat and potato stew, rice, and warm tortillas. A three-year-old boy showed me how to prep a warm tortilla with a little salt rolled up inside. All forty-three people sat around the six fold-out tables with the nuns, mothers, friends, and children in wheelchairs spaced around each. I watched Yoli's daughter, Ceci, an eleven-year-old with Down syndrome. She chatted and entertained the people at her table and had their smiling attention, waving her hands, standing up to demonstrate an action, and talking for most of the mealtime. Her movements and intonations mimic adult speech. Her words are invented sounds.

When we finished eating and the women were cleaning up, Ceci caught my eye. She walked over to me, took my hand, and led me to the worktable filled with colors and markers and coloring books. She selected pictures from the movie *Frozen* – Elsa for her and Anna for me. I colored as Ceci chatted and guided me to the area she wanted me to color and the color I was to use. When it was time for afternoon classes to start, I had a little trouble convincing Ceci that I couldn't attend class with her. The Sisters helped divert her attention, and every corner of the building was filled with activities for the afternoon sessions.

~ 4 ~

CUCA

I was waiting for Cuca in the small workshop on Inéz's land in Anapra where the prayer flags are made. Sara was setting up the dyeing and cutting equipment. Cuca entered with Angel, her eleven-year-old son. The handsome sixth grader was leaning on Cuca's arm to help him navigate the three steps into the workshop. Heavy braces supported his underdeveloped legs. He lifted himself into a chair, and Cuca gave him her cell phone to play a game. Then she told me her story.

"My early memories are working the cornfields with my little sister. One time, I pinched her hard, on the thigh. She let out a scream and kept screaming. Finally, Papá yelled at me to take her back to the house. I pinched her again, so she kept crying until we were out of the sun.

"We were so poor. I think that made Papá angry. He and Mamá would fight, split up, and get back together. We never visited friends, never went to parties. Never a piñata, no hugs or kisses. It was just plant seeds, cut corn, plow the field, carry water, scrub clothes at the river, make fire, grind corn.

"When I was old enough to go to school, it was a gift, an escape from the labor, and I had books. I loved the books. Papá let us go to school, but after third grade he pulled the boys out. 'No book will teach you to work the land, how to care for a cow, make adobe bricks, build a fence, manage a field of corn.'

"My teacher wanted me to stay in school. He begged Papá, and he allowed me to stay through fifth grade. It took three years to finish fifth grade because Papá kept taking me out of school to work the field. I was smart. I won second place in a whole school competition, and the teacher was going to take the top three winners to another town to compete for the prize. They even gave me money for the trip. 'No,' Papá said. 'It is not for you. You need to take care of the cows.'

"Felix was a handsome boy who lived on a *ranchito* nearby. Our families had been enemies for generations. Some great uncle killed another great uncle, or that's what they said. I didn't really know Felix well, but when our eyes met outside the church one day, we had feelings. Eventually, Felix talked to Papá. He still hated their family, but he needed to marry me off. Papá had to pay for my church wedding."

TORTILLAS FULL OF ANGER

"Did it get better? No. My mother-in-law squeezed the dreams from my life. [Cuca wrung her hands]. Mother-in-law insisted we get married in a church in the neighboring community. The trip was too expensive, so only a few from my family could come. There was no celebration, just a drive back to his family's little *ranchito* where I was installed as the maid, no, really, the slave! She demanded that I take over most of the housework: get up early, clean the fire pit, make the fire, walk half a mile to the well and carry back the big bucket of water on my head, make tortillas, wash the clothes in the river, get firewood, do all the cleaning. Mother-in-law helped a little, but in a house full of sons, no one else helped. In fact, I had to help them with the cows or the corn fields.

"I got pregnant right away and worked until the day the baby was born. The next day, Mother-in-law's words were, 'We are like chickens here. We lay the egg and get back to work.' I was back at work full-time.

"Usually, after a baby, there is a little celebration. I had no one to talk to, no friend to give me an *atole* to drink to celebrate the baby. 'We are poor here,' Mother-in-law said. 'You knew that when you married.'

"We had sex, but no love. There was no love at all in that house. Felix liked to make eyes at other women and make bruises on me. The neighbors could see what was going on. One woman tried to give me a little financial support, paying me to do some laundry. I hauled both loads of laundry to the river, pounded the laundry on the rocks, and returned to Felix's demand to help work the cows in the field. Always with the baby.

"I never knew why or when he would hit me. Anything would make him explode. Once, he hit me with a broom stick in front of his mother. Mother-in-law just crossed her arms in front of her chest and did not say a single word to stop him.

"I didn't want to live like this. I was stuck there, making the tortillas full of anger and hate, for six years. Then I heard about jobs in the factories in Juárez and begged Felix to move north. 'We can have our own family there. I can work too. It will be nice. Please, can we leave here? We can live under some tree. That will be better.' No. He loved his ranch.

"And then, in 1995, we did move to Juárez. His whole family came too. They sold the cattle, sold the farm, everything. They built a house here, and out back, Felix and I lived in a tiny house of packing pallets and tarpaper – really just a shack with a dirt floor. I had nothing of my own. Not a pot nor a blanket. I had to borrow, go begging for everything from Mother-in-law. Juárez was much colder than Durango, and the little shack had no heater; so we would sleep in Mother-in-law's house, on the floor, in the winter. But at least at times there was a wall, a thin wall, between us and the evil that flowed from the woman."

MY TEARS CAME SLOWER THERE

Then, there were many jobs in the maquiladoras. Not much pay, not easy, not fun. But after what Cuca had been through, it was welcomed. Her first job was in the Coilcraft factory making electronic harnesses for cars. Most of Felix's brothers found jobs also, and a sister-in-law watched the kids. Cuca worked from 6:00 a.m. until 3:30 p.m. six days a week. She had a little peace. With her third pregnancy, she was still working all day and caring for two little children. The babies were cranky and did not sleep much.

"The women who worked with me, we became good friends, especially Maggie who saw I was sick and worn down. Maggie asked the woman who ran the assembly line if she could work during her break so I could take a little nap in the bathroom.

"Felix worked, too, at a store. But he spent his money buying good clothes for himself and going to parties. He bought a little food for us, but really didn't help much. When the baby was born, I had to stay in that little shack. Mother-in-law wouldn't let me go to the big house. 'The kids would destroy my things!' Little Magda called it a house for pigs, and we were always hungry.

"One day, Felix's brother came into the shack with a chicken – one of the few times anyone in the family shared food. I made chicken soup. Pablo, my second child, was just about five years old. He liked the soup and a little while later, he went to the bathroom. 'It hurts when I make pee pee,' he cried. I went to Mother-in-law and said, 'Where is Felix?'

"'Why do you want him?' she asked.

"'Pablo is sick.'

"'Well,' I said, 'I haven't seen him since I gave him the hundred pesos.'

"Later, Felix came in with a gallon of milk. I asked him, 'Is that all you bought? Where is the rest of the 100 pesos?' He got mad, dumped the milk on the floor, and left.

"The next day, one of my sisters-in-law whispered to me. 'The chicken Felipe gave you was a black chicken. That is why Pablo got sick.' (Some indigenous customs involve using a chicken or egg to absorb the evil or the illness from a loved-one's body. That chicken then becomes a black chicken.)

"When the baby was one year old, I went back to work, again on the assembly line making electronic harnesses for cars. This was a good place to work – good friends there, one free meal, and transportation. I worked the night shift so little Magda, who was just ten years old, could take care of her little brother, Pablo, and the new baby at night.

"Magda hated it and cried so much. '*Mamí,* we are so hungry.' I worked hard in the factory so I wouldn't think of the little babies. My tears came slower there.

"Felix got worse. His life was his *ranchito*, and now he worked in a factory. He was mad all the time. I wanted so much to go to a little dance or take the kids to town to share an ice cream or something. That never happened. So, I danced with the kids outside in the sand, and we were happy when he left us alone.

"Felix quit coming home most nights. He didn't give us any money. He never hit the kids, but he hit me. One time, it was four in the morning, and he came banging on the door. I let him in. He laid down on the little cot and ordered me to take off his boots. 'I can't now. I'm feeding the baby.'

"He went into a rage and slammed me to the wall. Magda took the baby and ran out of the house – alone out in the dark. Little Pablo, who had just graduated from kindergarten, jumped on his daddy's back, and screamed, 'Don't hit my mamá!'

"I went to work wearing sunglasses to hide my purple eyes. 'I fell down,' I told the boss.

"He goes, 'You didn't fall down. He hit you.'

"The evil was spreading to the children. Magda had a boyfriend who was being mean to her. Little Pablo started being aggressive with me and the baby."

A BAD THING TURNED INTO A GOOD THING

One day, the factory hosted a counselor from a women's shelter, Las Hormigas, to talk to the employees. Apparently, Cuca wasn't the only one who "fell down a lot." The counselors talked to the employees about self-esteem, a woman's value, and the laws against abuse. Las Hormigas offered help. Cuca and her children went to the shelter every Saturday. The children went to the school and Cuca went to therapy with the counselor and other women from the factories. They encouraged her to leave the abuse. But she stayed with Felix. Then, as Cuca described it, "A bad thing turned into a good thing."

It was a hot August day. One of Felix's brothers bought rifles in El Paso and smuggled them across the border. The brothers were excited because they could take the guns to Durango and sell them and get a lot of money. So, that night they were partying and drinking. They started shooting the guns in the air to celebrate. The police came. Felix took off running, but they caught him. They put all four of the brothers in prison. Two of the brothers had money and paid to get out. His mother paid for the other brother to get out so he could take care of his kids. But not Felix. She would not help him, and Cuca couldn't. He was sentenced to ten years in the Juárez prison, and his family abandoned him.

"He had a pretty good room because if you are in prison there you can work in a maquiladora and pay for some things, and he took the factory job. I thought, well, the family is gone, maybe we could start new. I would be a good wife, and three times a week I rode the bus to visit him, to take him his favorite food and his clothes clean and ironed.

"Then he got his girlfriend pregnant with her second baby while he was in prison. That made me mad, and I finally took some action. I went back to the Las Hormigas counseling sessions and realized I had a sickness also, an addiction to the pain. The psychologist told me, 'You are good. You can break free. What do you want for your future?' Well, I wanted to separate from all that painful past. They had lawyers there, and they helped me get a divorce."

Divorce was a huge step for Cuca. Felix's brothers hounded her, saying, "You can't divorce. It is your obligation. You were married in the church."

She talked to a priest. The priest, a wise old man, said, "No one has to endure beatings and abuses."

"Felix told me, 'If you leave, I'll hunt you down and I'll kill you.' I was afraid, but now I knew that was part of breaking the addiction."

PANCHO VILLA'S GRANDDAUGHTER

Through all her experiences with Felix, Cuca was still working at the maquiladora. But that factory was shutting down. They gave her the equivalent of about $800 U.S. dollars as a severance payment. Felix's family went back to Durango, so Cuca was staying in their house. She saved her money and began planning how she would escape.

She divorced Felix and left him alone in prison. She left that house full of its memories of hate and violence. With the severance from the factory, she bought a small plot of land in Anapra, more sand than land, but it was her own place. She bought some building materials on credit and built the first room of wood and packing pallets. She and Magda stayed up most of the night painting their first room.

It was still hard. They were alone and they had very little. She continued to work, and Magda watched the little ones in the evenings. Her new job was at a factory making small components for electric appliances such as heaters, thermostats, and small electric circuit boards. Employees were required to wear a hat, shoe covers, apron, and no jewelry. Everything had to be clean. Some jobs required the use of chemicals like acetone to clean the components. Cuca was soldering the tiny components. Any woman who was pregnant was required to work in a special line away from the chemicals, so they moved her.

"You know, there were three women who applied for that job. The other two had their education and papers. I didn't. They hired me. Maybe they thought I would be quiet. But I'm not. I'm a good fighter, maybe I'm Pancho Villa's granddaughter! If something is wrong or they are not treating someone well, I let the boss know. They don't fire me, but I never win the best employee award![3]

"Now, I was pregnant with Angel. The factory managers were still hard on me. I went for my sonogram. I saw a funny look on the technician's face. I said, 'What is it? What do you see?'"

"Oh nothing, Senora." Then he wrote it down on the

---

[3] Pancho Villa inspired Cuca. There was quite an upheaval in Mexico around 1910 when political leaders led efforts to overthrow an unpopular dictator, Porfirio Diaz. Two Mexicans who led the resistance, Emiliano Zapata and Pancho Villa, became heroes. Pancho Villa led the northern resistance and spent much time in Cuidad Juárez.

form. I didn't understand it, so I took it to work with me and showed the nurse. She read it and told me I would have to have a Cesarean to deliver him. It was spina bifida. The baby had an eleven-centimeter growth on his lower spine. The doctor said it was my fault for not taking folic acid."

Sara was in the prayer flags workshop with us preparing the dyes and not interfering with out interview. However, when she heard that, she interrupted, "Every doctor tells the women it is their fault. Here in Anapra there is a high concentration of babies with spina bifida. It is not the folic acid, and it is not their fault!" Mexican doctors and clinics regularly give folic acid to pregnant women as part of normal treatment.

"I was depressed but kept looking for other opinions. A younger doctor with more experience explained that it was a bubble in the placenta, and it was not my fault. God doesn't send these babies to just anyone, but to those who know how to care for them and love them. I had to keep working in the factory, but they did give me the maternity leave that all workers get by law – thirty-five days before and thirty-five days after the birth.

"I went into labor and went to the hospital. That doctor. I still remember his face. He told me, 'The Tarahumara women, [4] when they have a baby with spina bifida, they don't have to have a Cesarean. You can deliver normally.'

"Three days! Three days of labor. Finally, a nurse, I

---

[4] Tarahumara or Raramuri are an indigenous people in the mountain areas of northern Mexico. Some have relocated to a community in southern Juárez.

remember her face too. A kind face. She came in and found out that the doctor didn't want to do a Cesarean, and she said to that doctor, 'This woman is going to have a Cesarean right now.' He did the surgery. My social security paid for it, although I had to fight to prove that I was eligible for the benefits."

A few years after Angel was born, Magda was old enough to work in the factories. The boys were old enough to care for Angel when he was small, so Magda and Cuca worked together in the factories; hopping from one to another to dodge the shutdowns.

"Sometimes the older women [on the line] give me advice, and sometimes I give advice and comfort to the new girls. We become good friends. Sometimes we have to raise our hands for permission to go to the bathroom. Ha! My bladder is not educated to tell time! You know, we just don't drink water. That's not good for our kidneys. Then you take the long bus ride home and sometimes I am about to burst!

"I run to get everything done for the kids. Run to catch the bus. Then run, run, run at the factory. I make my quotas every day. I do a thousand packages in one day – more than the morning shift ever does.

"I'm Pancho Villa's granddaughter here too. There was a big Mexican festival on March twenty-first. The boss said we have to work that day. I told her, 'No, it's a national holiday. If we work on a holiday you are supposed to give us triple salary.' Well, at least she said she'd give us double salary.

"The middle level management invent rules. If we are sick, we go to work so they won't dock our pay. Every day's pay [about $8.00 in this factory] we need to live on. Music is not permitted in the factory nor on the bus. We need our music, and that is just their way to make us leave the job so they can give it to younger workers. They told us we would get a bonus if we increased production. We did increase production. No bonus ever came."

I LIVE LIFE BETTER NOW

Cuca's financial stress is still very real; but now, she can manage. She helps with the Guerilla Prayer Flags and gets a little income to help with the expensive diapers for Angel. A few years ago, a church group from Kansas came and built two more rooms onto her house. Felix got out of jail and crossed to work in the United States. At the time of our interview, he was in Oklahoma, working in a car dealership. He has another family there. But he still communicates with Cuca, and he sends money to the kids. She says she has forgiven him and credits her God for this ability. Felix told her he is proud of the children and thanked her for all she did for them.

Magda is married with two children and works at S-Mart in Anapra. Cuca watches Magda's children (ages seven and three) during the day and then works her factory shift at night. Pablo went to Oklahoma to live with Felix. Felix even bought a car for his son.

"Finally, a little love came into my world. I am proud of my family. I communicate with my parents and brothers and sisters, and I feel something special for all of them. They all call on me when they have some problem and I always try to be there to help them when I can. Thanks to God's abundant blessings I know good people and live modestly in my house. I have the necessities, health, work. I like traveling. I'm going to visit my brothers across the border, and in three weeks they're promoting me to a higher job in my work with a better salary. Like the Bible says, 'Sow seeds of goodness and reap joy.' This is how I live life better now."

~ 5 ~

MINERVA

It was my first visit with Minerva. I was trying to find her house among the sandy lanes, and my car got stuck in one of the sand-trap roads. I got out of the car and walked around it feeling absolutely desperate. A young man from the house nearby came running out with some old carpet strips and a shovel. He smiled at me, set the carpet strips under my back wheels, shoveled out the ruts, and soon I was on my way. It stings my heart to tell that story because I didn't have any cash to give him. He gave me a very valuable gift, and a twenty-dollar bill would have been five days' pay for him.

Years ago, Minerva's husband and his brother combined resources and brought a plot of land in Anapra about a mile up the sandy hills from the main street. Over these years, each brother built his own house on the land, one room at a time. A sturdy fence with a wrought iron gate surrounds the two houses and the small front concrete patio where children's wheeled toys are parked. Minerva's house looks similar to some homes in the U.S. with an ample kitchen and basic appliances. There are two bedrooms and a small bathroom for the family of six. The floor is made of shiny white tiles. The front door and dining furniture are heavy-lacquered carved wood.

Ornaments decorate the walls. It is a home of pride.

Their home was not always this nice. The brothers moved to this plot when land in Anapra was very inexpensive, when the maquiladora owners were trying to woo workers. The first buildings were small, temporary shelters. Over time, they gathered more materials and added rooms. The two families still support each other with shared meals, shopping, transportation, and child-care.

I sat on the velour couch and Minerva served me coffee. Her children joined us. The thirteen and nine-year-old daughters sat with me on the couch, trying not to stare at the big white woman. The four-year-old twins played with little wheeled toys on the living room floor. The children roamed in and out.

She sat down in the chair beside me and pointed to a picture of her and her husband displayed on the corner table – a very attractive couple. "That is our wedding picture. We didn't have money to get married, but we went to a friend's wedding and took that picture. We say that is our wedding." She laughed and gently slid her finger across their faces. "He still leaves little gifts for me."

"Now, let me tell you my story, and you tell this story to other people. My story should be a movie!"

She seemed in a trance, never flinching, not distracted by the children in the room.

"I remember when we moved to the big city, Gómez Palacio, there was my mamá, papá, my big sister, Julia, and her little boy. We got a little piece of land right at the city dump. Papá bought a cart – an old wooden cart with big wheels. Every morning, Mamá filled it with fruits and sweets, and sometimes, if Papá caught any fish in the early morning, there were fish to sell. Papá grabbed the metal bar and pushed the heavy cart through the streets selling what he could. Sometimes he worked in the fields picking cotton or chile. That is what we lived on."

While Papá was working, Julia and Minerva dug bricks out of a dump. After a few months, they had enough bricks to build one room. As soon as she was old enough, Minerva worked – sweeping streets, helping neighbors clean their houses, helping her papá. But she never missed school until she was thirteen, when life became more difficult.

Julia had left them and crossed into the United States, leaving the little boy with the family. They didn't hear from her for three years. Then she came to visit with twin babies. She left them with Papá and Mamá, and crossed back to the U.S. Papá became ill, paralyzed for an unknown reason. They had no money.

"The responsibility fell on my back, such a little girl, just thirteen. So, I started to work in a maquiladora in Gómez Palacio. I wasn't really old enough, but my friend knew the boss. They needed workers and he made the paperwork to sign me up. I worked from eight a.m. until six p.m. and then, if I had any money, I caught a bus to a high school which had evening classes. Sometimes I had to walk, and it was a long way, but, still, I was going to school. My dream was to be a nurse."

THE MOVE TO JUÁREZ

A few years later, Julia crossed back over the border to her parents' home. She stayed a few days and then left, taking her three children to Juárez where she lived with a man she called her husband. Then Mamá became ill. The parents decided they had to move to Juárez to be with Julia, hoping she could help them. They packed all they could carry and got on the bus to Juárez. When they found Julia, she was living in a shed made of corrugated metal, a place where a man had kept dogs. It was filthy. Julia had put the three children in a free government shelter so she could work in the factories. The shelter had too many children and poor care.

"When we got to that school, Julia's little boy came running up to me and hugged me and cried, 'Please take us out of here!' The babies were filthy, and flies were all over the baby bottles."

Now, Papá and Mamá (both ill), Julia, Minerva, the little boy, and two babies were all living in that shed. Julia was working two shifts in a factory and Minerva found a job in a restaurant.

"I got good tips because I took the little boy. He was seven years old and so cute. He dressed up like a waiter and helped me serve the customers. They loved him because he was so cute, and they gave us good tips. I couldn't go back to school because I had to work all the time."

When Minerva was sixteen, she found a job in a maquiladora. The pay was a little better than the restaurant, and she had health benefits and social security. Of course, that was not enough to meet the family's needs. Julia worked, but she had trouble keeping her jobs. Minerva was the one who had to make the money. It just was not enough for the family. The little ones needed diapers and milk and much more.

AN ENORMOUS FROSTED CUPCAKE

Gloria Steinem said, "The United States is an enormous, frosted cupcake in the midst of millions of starving people." Minerva nibbled on the cupcake.

"I had a friend from the maquiladora, Lola, who was a little wild, a *chola*. Her father had drinking problems. Lola had no money either. She had been asking me to cross the border with her to go to *el Norte* to try to get money. My family would not approve, so I said no. But things got desperate, and I had to get food for the family.

"One morning, I got up very early, dressed in baggy clothes with my hair all messy so I looked ugly...you know, so the men wouldn't notice me. I went to Lola's house, and we walked across the border. That was in the 1980s, and you could cross then, through the creosote bushes and the sand, over there on the edge of Anapra. We walked to an area where there were some nice houses and asked if we could clean the house or wash the dishes. Some people were nice and let us work and paid us. They gave us used clothes and food. On the way back, I bought powdered eggs. We had not eaten eggs in months.

"We got home late that night and put everything on Lola's bed and divided it evenly. When I got home, Mamá was mad. 'Where have you been all day?' I showed her all the stuff and the thirty-five dollars. We had a late-night party, and the babies had milk in their bottles.

"Soon I got a better job in another maquiladora. I worked there five days a week, and Lola and I crossed on the weekends. We learned how to hitch a ride to a little bigger community, Anthony, and the managers of the grocery story let us carry groceries to the cars, and people gave us tips. Some people gave us groceries and used clothes. Lola kept one of the grocery carts, and we stashed the stuff in the cart and waited. When evening came, we pushed it over the border. Most of the time, if *La Migra* [the border patrol agent] saw us, they just looked the other way. But sometimes we got in trouble. Once they took us to the Border Patrol office, confiscated our haul, took our fingerprints, and sent us back over the border. We waited a few weeks and crossed again. During those months, we had extra food, cash, and clothes because we crossed.

"Then, one day, the owner of a restaurant took us inside his place. He gave us a nice plate of Mexican food. He sat with us and said, 'My family lives in Juárez. Can you help them cross the border? I can pay you sixty dollars per person – there are four of them.'

"I was scared. Slipping over to do odd jobs was one thing, but being a *coyote*, a human smuggler – that was dangerous.

"Lola liked the idea, and she helped the man and got his family over the border. Then her business expanded, she involved her friends and her cousins, and eventually she added drugs to her border crossings. Lola was able to buy a nice house in the Mexican state of Nayarit, but they eventually caught her and now she's in jail."

Minerva wanted to keep working on her dream to be a nurse. With the money she made at the maquiladora, she could go to school and still help her family. One school allowed students to get their nursing certificates in one year. She paid for that herself.

"No one ever helped me. No one! When I told my mamá I was in school, she said, 'That's good.' But, you know, that was the happiest time of my life. I was working on my dream! I loved anatomy. I did well in the classes. I could not pay all the fees, so I had to drop out of the school. But I did get the Red Cross training. You get the training, you get your certificate, and then you work for Red Cross for three years. There is no pay, but it is a very rewarding and fun experience. I loved it so much."

THIRTY DAYS OF LOVE

"Then, Mamá became very ill. She called me to her bedside and told me this story.

'Mija, Julia is not your sister. She is your mother. When we lived on the ranchito in Durango, Julia was very smart in school. She needed to go to a good high school, so we sent her to live with her cousin in Gómez Palacio. Julia was in the last year of a pre-med in a specialized high school. She would have entered medical school the next year.

'Your papá and I went to see her. Julia stood with her hands like this [she crossed her arms in front of her stomach], and she was wearing baggy clothes. I said, "Are you pregnant?" She started crying.

Your papá went crazy with rage. He called her a whore. He said he would never give her another penny. And he said she was not his daughter. I was angry too, but I felt sorry for her. We just left her there on her own. Then, she kept going off with different men and having babies. And you know how she is now.

'I am so sick now, Mija. But your mother, Julia, is very sick also. Go see her.'

"I was living here in our little two-room house with my husband and baby Mariela. I felt this anxiety in my chest. I needed to see my mother, my real mother. It was the week of Easter, and I had a few days off. It was so cold; no buses were running. I had only fifty pesos. I was crying uncontrollably. My sister-in-law said, 'I'll go with you.' So, we walked – several miles in the dark.

"When I finally arrived, Julia had blood in her eyes. Her neighbor had a car but he wanted us to pay for the gas. I gave him all the money I had, and he took us to the clinic. They took her in and wanted seventy-five pesos for the consultation. How was I going to get money for that? After a few days, the doctor told us she might die tomorrow or in three months. She had AIDS and tuberculosis. He said I could take her home.

"Well, they won't let you out of the hospital until you pay your bills, and they keep charging you while you are in the hospital. We didn't have the money to get her out of the hospital. I called Uncle Juan, Papá's little brother. He has a good job with some retirement business across Mexico, and he has some money. He paid to get her out.

"We took her to her house. You know, I had never given my mother a Mother's Day gift, and that day we took her home, it was May tenth. I wanted to give her something, but we had nothing. The maquiladora where I worked had a rose garden. My friend took me to the factory, and I cut some roses and took them to her. She kept those roses in her arm – even when they were dry and dead. She died on May 30 with those roses in her arms.

"I told her I loved her; the past was not important. Then she started telling me what happened when she got pregnant with me. She and her cousin were in the city, Gómez Palacio, living with friends so they could go to school. They were both in high school. Her cousin said, 'Let's go to a party.' So, they went. There was drinking, maybe drugs. The cousin said they would go to a hotel after the party. Julia must have been drugged or maybe drunk. They went to the hotel. The cousin brought a man to the hotel. Julia told me she did not remember anything, but she woke up and was in a lot of pain. Her cousin never said anything about what happened.

"She hated me and tried many ways to get me out – to abort me. I had ruined her life. She wanted to be a doctor, and now, she was helpless and worthless. I guess God wanted me to stay because I had to take care of her children. Well, after I was born, she gave me to my grandparents, and she went with a man who was older, and they went to the U.S. She had several men and several children. I guess she felt like she was a whore.

"She rejected me, and now I understand why she never liked me. I was the result of her rape. But, in those thirty days, she gave me all her love. She died on May 30 and I was holding her hand and she was holding her dry roses. My grandmother-mother died a week later.

"I thought of all we had missed together, and the pain was so deep. I broke down. I couldn't understand why she died like this. I dreamed of her every day. I returned to my little house and went to bed in severe depression. My husband was worried. He took me to a ranch to try to get me out of the depression, but I started feeling all the symptoms of my mamá. I know it was in my mind, but I really felt it. We came back to Juárez and he took me dancing. But the music was loud, and the rhythm hurt my lungs. We went to the doctor. He said I wasn't sick, but if I kept on like that, I would really get sick.

"I didn't want to live. I just sat in my house rocking back and forth thinking of ways I could kill all of us, my husband, baby, and me. I didn't want to leave them; I wanted them to die with me. I was trying to think of how to poison their drink.

"Finally, one day I woke up and said, 'Ya! Enough! That's it!' I got up, cleaned the house, and took a bath and got dressed. I went to Las Hormigas. I went to their counseling. Mariela got to go to the Las Hormigas School. I was learning that I was sick. They helped me get better. I went to work in a new maquiladora and started taking care of my family. And I thought, 'How marvelous is life!'

"Well, because of that, I now have a better understanding of depression. I know the person can't control it. So, when we are at work on the factory line, if someone has a problem... well, we all have problems...but they know they can talk to me. I really don't know what to say, but I listen. They need to talk out their problems. One of the girls makes fun of someone who is depressed. I tell her not to. I remember what it was like.

"Now I can talk about it. I can see that I really have deep sorrow for my mother – how not just her body was raped, but also her future and her dreams were raped. For many years, I hated that cousin. I will never know what really happened, but I think she sold my sister to that man. I didn't talk to her for years. Finally, I thought, who am I to judge her? I have my own errors. In the end, she is my cousin, so just forget it."

YOU CAN'T BUY BREAD WITH AN APRON

When Minerva was better, she worked in a factory making parts for automobiles and the aerospace industry receiving almost $45.00 per week. Her job was on the line near the radiation machine. They were able to pay off debts and build a little more onto their house. Soon, she was pregnant with another baby. In the fourth month, the doctor told her the baby had no kidneys. She was crying as she told me about the baby.

"I didn't believe him and went to the best childbirth doctor in town. He said, 'Don't waste your money. The baby will die. He has no kidneys. His lungs will fill up with water and he will die.' They said it would be best to abort the baby, but I could feel him living in me, so I kept him. I talked to the baby a lot. I told him we could not be together physically, but he was always with me spiritually. I was afraid he was deformed. I never got to see the baby, but my husband did. He said he was not deformed. Two other women were pregnant at the same time as I was. One of them had a baby who also died, and the other one had a baby that was sick.

"Later, I went to apply for a job at Foxconn. I was just going to pick up the application, so I was dressed in jeans and flip flops. They told me, 'The bus will pick you up and take you to the factory for an interview now. It's okay if you're not dressed.' I thought, well, okay I'll go. I did the interview, then they did a medical exam testing for pregnancy, high blood pressure, and high blood sugar. You cannot work there if you don't pass those tests.

"I went on my first day. It was horrible! They made all of us new employees stand in a line. Just stand there, straight, for eight hours! No breaks! The Chinos [Foxconn is a Chinese-owned technology production operation] are very strict. They treat us like soldiers. I do not like the way they treat us. But there is no other option now. They give only one meal and it is not very good. Just pasta, soup, refried beans. I am easy to please, so I eat the food.

"And there are so many employees. It takes eighty-nine *ruteros* [bus routes] just to get us there and back for all the shifts. Most people come and go. My husband works there. He usually works the early morning shifts and weekends. He is the maintenance man for the line." (There are three shifts per day at the large maquiladoras. It can take thirty bus routes per shift to get the employees to the factories on time – over a thousand employees per shift.)

"They make only Dell computers. They have thirteen manufacturing lines and there are one hundred people working on each line. Then there are many other people around the factory doing other jobs. At the start it is assembly, then testing the machines, then another round of testing, then packaging. Each line produces two hundred computers per hour. I work at the start – the assembly part. I get [$59 U.S.] per week. I get thirty minutes for lunch. I get extra [$13 U.S.] overtime pay if I take a night shift.

"It was really hard the first two years. You stand all day. Never get to sit and rest. Now my body is accustomed to it. The schedule is not set. That makes it very difficult. I'll go in on Monday at three-thirty p.m., and I should work until one-thirty a.m. But, when I get there, they may tell me, 'We need you to work through the night until seven-thirty in the morning.' If I say I can't work then, they'll say, 'Well, there are many people who want jobs if you don't want to do it.' We have to keep working until the next bus shift comes in to take us home. We do get paid for the extra time. Sometimes, I go with only maybe three hours of sleep for the whole day. Sometimes, they tell me to come in the next day and work eight to three; sometimes six-thirty in the afternoon to six-thirty the next morning. It's hard to plan my life and get milk for the little ones!

"Now I can do the math. There is very little overhead. They don't use much electricity like other factories. With two hundred computers coming off each of the thirteen lines each hour, and computers cost a lot in the store, and little overhead, and the little they pay us; they are getting a lot of money for themselves! They could give us a better salary or better food, or maybe some parties. You know what we got for Cinco de Mayo? We got a little bag of chips and a coke. We had a party, just for one hour, where we could sing karaoke. Why not a nice party? We give a lot to them, why don't they give back a little. No, they are very demanding.

"Most of the people on the line are women. Most people come and go. Just a few of us have been there as long as my five years. There is an infirmary and a nice nurse. But she can't do anything. They won't give you any kind of medicine. There is no ambulance for any emergency. One time a man got a bad cut on his ankle. They just gave him a tub to put his foot in for all the blood and someone drove him to the hospital in a car. If you get sick, you just have to keep working or sit in the infirmary until your bus route comes back. They say there is a doctor, but I have never seen him.

"I feel like they treat us like burros or robots. Almost no raises, no nice things. We only get a few holidays. We get eight days off each year after we have been there a full year. They do not provide any support for education at all. I was there for two years before I got a raise. I did get a higher job, but it was just with more responsibility and a different color apron, no extra money. I can't buy bread with the new apron!"

~ 6 ~

THE ANTS AND THE EX-NUNS

Honey mesquite is common in this part of the Chihuahua Desert. In late summer, the small tree drops its bean pods; the beans inside are sweet to taste. On my walks, I often see three or four ants carrying a piece of mesquite bean pod to their home. The pod is five or six times larger than the ants and much heavier than their combined weight. Just making the journey to cross the road can take fifteen minutes. They work in unison and they persist.

Most of the women who participated in this research mentioned a support center in Anapra that provided help during some of their most difficult times. That center has existed for two decades and is called The Ants, in English, Las Hormigas, in Spanish. As the directors told me, "The processes of social change are slow and steady, like the ants doing their work, caring for their community. Ants in community development. Our community is always in development."

The website, www.lashormigascommunity.org/ingles /index.html presents this mission statement: "We believe in the transformation of people who live in poverty, accompanying them in their growth and self-awareness process toward a more dignified, healthy, and harmonious reality. In return, they will transform their families and their communities."

The facility is made from adobe block with five large trees framing the front walk, the parking area, and the steps up to the porch. It is located on one of the sandy streets on the western end of Anapra. Visitors must ring the doorbell to be admitted through the locked doors. Inside, real and artificial plants, colorful paintings, and padded chairs accent the reception area where an employee provides a gracious welcome. Down a hall to the left of the reception area is the office for the two directors, Elvia Villescas and Linabel Sarlat, with their desks, a small conference table, and shelves loaded with books and supplies. A window provides a view of the front porch and front door, and another window gives a view of the street. Further down this hall are three smaller rooms for individual counseling sessions. In the opposite direction from the reception is a large room used for group therapy sessions and meetings. Shelves are stocked with flyers about self-help and therapy practices. In the back is the large classroom set up for the Montessori-style learning, filled with well-designed tools and toys that allow children to learn through play. They are carefully organized to be accessible and welcoming to the children.

The directors shared their stories with me.

BECOMING NUNS AND EX-NUNS

Linabel: "I am of the Yucatan, from Merida. Yes, I have moved across Mexico from the far south to the far north.

[She laughs.] My father had a great respect for and love for the Maya women who came to our house. My older sister, well, I saw her give blessings to those women in a high poverty area in Merida. It was her mission. I was waiting at home to hear all about her experiences in that community – everything about their houses, their lives. It was in my soul even at that time. Later, when I was in Catholic school in primary grades, I went with the nuns to a low-income area in Merida. We stayed one week, living in their homes, talking with the people. We slept on the floor. It was important to live like they lived. It was marvelous. That is where I felt true happiness.

"There was a boy, my boyfriend. I told him I was thinking of becoming a nun. He said, 'You are going to have many children. Not from your womb, but from your spirit, from your heart.' Now, a good person from Yucatecan is romantic. It made me happy to think that I could be the wife of HIM [she raises her palms up], of Jesus. I watched the nuns as they were so interested in the people. And I wanted to live like that.

"So, I became a nun, always working with my sisters to do something beneficial for the people. Like the model of Jesus, his life, his love; or like Teresa, the Spanish nun who revolutionized the Carmelite order in the sixteenth century. My order was named after her – the *Teresianas*. I was happy for twenty-three years.

"Then, the years became difficult in our order [of nuns]. I was living here in Juárez. In 1998, our order was sent to a *colonia* [neighborhood] near the hill in the southern part of Juárez. We were working with the *Maristas*, nuns dedicated to education. They asked Elvia and me to create a high school for that community. We had to do everything – manage the construction, the curriculum, find the staff – everything. We worked on the school for years. It is still there, and it is a good school. I wrote all the units for the human development curriculum. They still use those lessons. The *Secretaría de Educatión* accepted our curriculum in human development. Then they sent us to other schools, schools in higher economic areas, to work with students there.

"I had a different vision than the authorities about this. I realized I did not have that happiness inside me. This was not what I wanted to do. I was in a difficult time as I was wanting to leave the nuns and to find a work with the low-income communities that I love. I wanted to live among the poor and work with the poor. I went to a convent in El Paso and stayed three days in silence trying to understand what to do.

"Elvia was in the same order of nuns with me. We knew each other, but we were not very close. Just as I was making this very difficult decision to leave the order, I learned Elvia was doing the same thing!"

I was impressed. "Really?" I asked.

"Yes! Yes! A blessing from God; we ended up on the same path and working together. In May it will be twenty years since we left the congregation. The blessing was that we were doing this together.

"When we announced that we were leaving the order, my older brother came to visit us and wanted to know if we were okay. My younger brother came, too. Elvia's parents came to check on her. They were worried. But they all left tranquil because we were okay. We wanted to do what was in our soul.

"There was a good friend, a priest here in Anapra,

Stanislaus Martinka. A great man. He has passed away. We have his obituary here. [Elvia reaches to a shelf and shows me the card from his funeral.] He was the one who got the money to build that high school. We were happy here, working with the people, learning from the community. Martinka loved all of Juárez. He was very interested in helping improve education here. He saw that we were living in some very small, rented rooms. He told us to look for a house, and we found one that had been vandalized, a mess, located in the middle of Anapra. Father Martinka bought that house and fixed it up for us. Thanks to him, we have a good house where we still live twenty years later.

"We had to decide what we wanted to do here in Anapra. There was so much, but we needed to find out from the people what was most important."

Elvia: "Yes, our decision to leave the sisterhood of the *Teresianas* was very difficult and painful, but our call was very clear – to live among the people in Anapra and to experience their uncertainty, their poverty, and their social realities. For this was the door to collaborate in the transformation of this social reality through serving their true needs.

"We were still working at the high school. Linabel was the coordinator. I was the principal. We decided to leave together. It would be so hard to leave alone. Who could do it alone? It was a form of support. What we wanted to do was work with the people who have no opportunities. Those who are not getting attention and support. There was no joy coming from the spiritual service at the high school. We knew our joy would come from the love we shared with Anapra. So, we went to Anapra. At that time, it was awful! So poor, ugly, full of poverty. No paved streets. No water.

"And, [she held up a hand and cocked her head] part of my soap opera is my relationship with a man who lives in San Francisco. Some of his colleagues provided support for our work, so when he came with them to Anapra, we fell in love. We were together for ten years. He is very involved in his work, and I am very involved here in Las Hormigas. We grew apart. Each of us must follow our own path. He is a very honorable man. I learned a lot from him."

LISTEN TO LEARN

As Linabel and Elvia became a part of the community and listened to the women, they saw several important issues in the community demanding attention. Those efforts were valuable, important steps that led them to their real place in the community. But their first effort did not accomplish its goal.

"One of the priests gave us three cows. The plan was to give the cows to three families that had been working with Las Hormigas improving their family life economically. However, all three families refused to take the gift cow. They did not have any money to purchase feed for the cow. We learned from that experience; and now our decisions for projects have to be made with the families so they can tell us what will work and what will not work."

Gang violence became atrocious in Juárez around 2009, and gang-related deaths in the city were at a global high. Particularly horrific were the kidnappings, tortures, sexual assaults, and murders of teenage girls and young women. When a body was found, attempts to identify the woman were mostly unsuccessful. In most cases, the girl's body was never found or identified. The families were left with the empty cruelty of never knowing. Young women in Ciudad Juárez (and around the globe) are still vulnerable, but those days were heartbreaking. Pink crosses commemorating each of the dead or missing girls are evident across the city, on fences, telephone poles, and walls. As you cross the downtown border bridge to return to El Paso, a large sculpture of wood and metal depicting the pink crosses and memorializing the young women is prominent on the column between the two traffic lanes.

Elvia and Linabel did what they could, mostly trying to provide comfort to the women whose daughters had been kidnapped or murdered, but, as Elvia told me, "Our commitment was to impact the living [she emphasized the word], the lives of women." And they were understanding that so many women in Anapra needed healing deep inside their hearts. In addition to the fear of being murdered, the young women in their community had been uprooted from their homes and families in the interior of Mexico, they had complex and abusive relationships with men who themselves were troubled, and they were working in a harsh environment in the factories, often worrying about the children they had to leave alone. Self-esteem and respect were stifled, and violence was nurtured. They needed a center for emotional healing and human development.

THE ANAPRA UBER

Linabel described one of the projects sponsored by Las Hormigas. This is the program Inéz referred to in her interview. Linabel's memory is slightly different.

"We understood that the women needed economic autonomy and that cooperation could help lead them to a life where they had money in their purse and didn't have to be asking a man. We received a donation of a used van. The women in our workshops, Inéz and Minerva and others, women with strong determination, told us that people had to walk from S-Mart up the sandy streets for sometimes two miles, carrying their groceries. Inéz and the women decided to use the van as an inexpensive Uber. Ha! They would take the people carrying the groceries to their homes for a small fee. The Uber was working very well, until the *rutero* drivers found out. The *rutero* drivers were afraid their van was taking away their customers. They were angry. They brought two of their big buses and surrounded the van. They dragged Inéz out and started beating her. A crowd of people who were coming out of S-Mart saw this, and they ran yelling at the *rutero* drivers, and those men left. But we knew they would harm the women if we continued our women to women transport.

"Then the women met to think of other ideas. They decided to make individual plates of food, and they would sell them out of that van while it was parked along the main street. It worked for a while until one of our volunteers crashed the van. Our little van died."

TRANSFORMATION COMES FROM INSIDE, SLOWLY

Elvia: "Through all of this, we could see that economic development, activism, and economic cooperatives were helpful, but we were not getting to the root of the problems. There was still envy, gossip, and competition. The women did not have self-respect, so they could not give respect. Ignorance, that lack of respect for women, low self-esteem, and *machismo* were cultivating violence against women and children. A lack of positive role models, open wounds for the loss of their homeland and their families when they moved north, these showed up in their cries, abuses, and broken communication.

"Those first two years in Anapra, we were learning and understanding the reality, how to work directly with the people. Then we knew that the development of the human being was missing – overcoming violence, defending your rights, financial sustainability. There was nothing about this in the schools."

Linabel: "The organizing and activism we had been doing did not fix their souls. The unresolved violence and suffering in the individual were going to affect the group. Social change is not going to work well without the deep change in the heart, the soul. You know, this is not what religions are doing now. Church is too often just about traditions, cults, and repetitions. To fix the problems, 'I will say catechism. I will pray for you.' [She shook her head to indicate no.]

"We believe the spiritual capacity of people is higher than religion and churches. It involves personal equality, gender equality, and living in peace and harmony. This work functions in a process of stages where the individuals decide what changes they are ready to make and when they want to accomplish those changes. We help them take small steps leading to the strength and knowledge necessary to make more healthy decisions.

"For example, there was a woman who came to us because her husband humiliated her, controlled her. He would not permit her to leave the house. He would go dancing, but she had to stay in the house. Then, through the therapy, she learned how to develop her voice. She learned she could look him in the eyes and say, 'I need to go see my mom.' Not asking permission but telling him. She learned such basics as how to use her voice and say things differently. Her husband was not violent, but he yelled, 'What are they teaching you at Las Hormigas.' She told him, 'I am going to see my mom. If you want to follow me, okay.' Finally, they separated. He left. I saw her a few years later, and she was alone but good, at peace. This story repeats many times. It's a common story."

Elvia added her comments. "We had to be trained to do this right. We went back for more education to do this work professionally with the highest quality programs. We now both have master's degrees in Gestalt psychotherapy and much training – some was international, like the workshop we took for several weeks in Guatemala. Linabel and I developed the curriculum and began providing workshops for women so they could work through their histories and the violence they had experienced. The transformation had to come from inside. Slowly."

Their friend, Father Martinka, found a donor who gave them the funds to build their center. Through the years, they have received financial support from foundations in the United States, Switzerland, and Germany, individual donations, Peace Development Fund, Catholic Charities, and others. In the first years, Linabel and Elvia visited with and learned from various organizations which specialized in developing human potential in high needs communities. They went through the legal processes to become an official Mexican Civil Association; allowing a reduction in taxes and businesses contributions to Mexican non-profits. The S-Mart grocery store in Anapra invites individuals, when they are paying at the register, to round up to the nearest bill, and those few extra *centavos* are donated to different charities. Interestingly, according to Linabel, most people do round up and donate. Las Hormigas has received funds from the S-Mart program over the years. They do not accept any government or political funding.

WOMEN ARE HELPING EACH OTHER NOW. WE HAVE LESS TO DO.

Las Hormigas has persisted with their mission, listening to the community, solving problems, and continually evolving to best meet the needs. Focusing on the family unit, they seek to improve attitudes and behaviors to reduce violence and aggression, and to overcome cognitive/emotional problems. The eleven employees, including four professional therapists, serve about 400 clients per month, including the children in their school. A recent evaluation of the program determined that the work of the center was relevant and valuable for the region, and that important changes in behavior resulted from a family's participation in the programs.

On that first visit to their office, I asked, "When you look out this window and you see a woman crying with her children, knocking on your door, what happens next?"

Linabel and Elvia looked at each other with puzzled expressions. After a few minutes, Elvia said, "You know, we don't see that anymore. I think it is because they have learned to come to us before problems get that bad. There is still violence. And so much poverty. But we think the men are feeling different. We have seen changes in the men; more respect for children."

Linabel added, "What we often hear now is how the women counsel each other. And do you know where that happens a lot? On the line in the maquiladoras! When they are working and talking, they are giving support and strength to each other. You know, the woman is the heart of Mexican culture. Everything spirals around her. When she fixes her own soul, that affects the whole group."

Elvia nodded. "There will be less darkness, less death. This is the dream. This is multiplying the light. Women are helping each other now. We have less to do."

A SUMMARY OF THE MODEL OF CARE AT LAS HORMIGAS

The directors shared their organizational documents with me. One key document, their Model of Care, a guide for funders and participants, explains how and why they use the counseling approaches they have implemented. The main focus of this Model of Care is human development, which is described in the document [through my translation] as "the capacity within the person to develop economically and to openly evolve physically, mentally, emotionally, and spiritually; to unblock thoughts and emotions and to embrace new learnings that bring about changes in old patterns, ultimately achieving a fuller, happier, and more harmonious life." The approach focuses around two axes: the therapeutic and the educative.

The therapeutic axis is based on accepted theoretical foundations and relevant research in the fields. The professionals at Las Hormigas work on the premise that the person, when immersed in their bio-psycho-socio-spiritual reality, is capable of restructuring to confront life experiences that led to their need for inner healing. Participants learn to confront their past, to claim it and own it and use it as the fuel driving them to control their peace and their futures.

The educative axis supports the center's vision of a future in which every child and adult develops their human potential and lives in harmony without violence. *Smiles in the Desert* is a school, although they don't like to use the word, school, or even education. Linabel described it. "We don't call it school because [she crossed her arms over her chest and squeezed them tight] the schools are so constricted, so controlling. We are educating them, working together to open their lives to more understand-ing and more positive growth. Learning is more of a partnership."

The Model of Care describes the method for teaching children. "Created by Maria Montessori, an educator, scientist, the first woman in Italy to graduate with a doctorate in medicine; as well as a psychologist, anthro-pologist, and philosopher. Inspired through working with the children in the highest poverty zones in Italy, she created a method of teaching-learning in which learning occurs through experience, using materials she created for this purpose that depict everyday life experiences." The Montessori educational model is structured for progress through developmental stages of socialization, respect, and cooperation.

There is evidence that the program has added strength and love in this community where physical comforts are scarce and the struggle for basic needs is as harsh as their desert wind. Linabel and Elvia state that they have drawn from many sources to stimulate the social development that has occurred and is occurring in Anapra – their work with religious groups, their education and experience, and ancestral and indigenous knowledge and practices. The one source that contributed most to the efforts was their collaborative approach to growth, drawing from their partnership with the community, listening and learning from their friends and neighbors, and adjusting their programs based in the wisdom in the hearts of the women they serve.

RELIGION'S FRACTURED ROLE IN COLONIZATION

Camilla Townsend[5] tells the history of the Spanish conquest from texts written by the Aztecs who documented their view of the conquest in their Nahuatl

[5] Camilla Townsend (2019). *Fifth Sun: A New History of the Aztecs.* Oxford University Press.

language. She worked with Nahuatl scholars who translated those ancient documents to provide a vital historic view.

In the early 1500s, Spain sent ships full of men with weapons and some basic supplies to Mexico (and most of the islands and lands of today's Central and South America, spreading into the Southwestern United States) to conquer the Indigenous peoples living there, take their lands, strip their natural resources, and establish their Spanish version of the Catholic religion. The Indigenous peoples were at best souls to be converted, all the while forced to serve the Spaniards as slaves, warriors, or captured sex providers. Within a few decades, the majority of the Indigenous peoples (80% to 90%) died from diseases the Spanish men brought with them. And, within several generations, the Indian slaves had built for the Spanish beautiful churches, homes, government houses, roads, and irrigation systems.

Eventually, the Indigenous peoples learned Spanish and most accepted a version of the Catholic religion. For good or bad, that religious intrusion became an organizing structure for society and has endured over the centuries.

Colonizing and religious oppression continued. Through marriage and rape, Spanish blood entered into the tribal groups. The Spanish aristocracy and priests created charts explaining the superiority of the blood mixtures (Mestizos) based on the quantity of male Spanish blood. There were some caring colonizers who tried to patch the worst social gashes left by the conquest, providing schools (for Spanish language and Catholic religion), health care, housing, and food. Priests who tried to move toward equity or justice, or to defend the

Indigenous' rights to their land were seldom successful.

Throughout that history, Catholics in Mexico, like the rest of us, acted sometimes through egoism and sometimes through altruism. In the mid-1900s, some Catholics in Latin America, gravitating toward liberation theology, understood that the economic privilege that empowered the conquerors and their descendants had forced oppression and poverty on generations of the Mestizo. Many priests and nuns embed benevolent efforts in their understandings of social justice. That is evident in these transformations we see in Anapra.

~ 7 ~

DR. MENDOZA

Mary Alice Scott is a medical anthropologist at New Mexico State University. She has led fundraisers for women's support centers in Ciudad Juárez, especially helping cancer patients get access to the treatment they need. She joined me on three of the interviews with Minerva and Cuca. Over coffee one morning, she mentioned hearing of a doctor in Ciudad Juárez who worked in a clinic that was actually located on the solid waste landfill – on the dump. Millions of tons of waste are unloaded in this desert area south of the city. Although the waste is covered with sand, the disposal site does not meet standards for U.S. waste facilities. Some Mexicans survive by rummaging through the waste for items to repurpose or sell. As we investigated further, we discovered that this doctor had another clinic located in Anapra. It had been functioning for decades providing vital affordable services to the residents.

Mary Alice and I arranged a visit, and Dr. Mendoza showed us her facility in Anapra and let us visit with her small staff and some of her patients in the waiting room. Through the years she has found funding to provide vital help to people living on the edges of the city and on the edges of health and safety. She has negotiated U.S. and

Mexican legal and civil regulations to ensure that these folks have good medical care and vital supplies. I knew that her story was part of the foundation of Anapra, and it should be told.

A general practitioner, Dr. San Juana Mendoza has provided medical assistance to the most vulnerable people in Ciudad Juárez for more than thirty years, reaching from 2,500 up to 3,000 per year. One of her most successful programs is in Anapra. This is managed through her Mexican Civil Association, a non-profit named *Una Familia por México, A.C.* The mission is "outreach to the vulnerable – uneducated, low income, orphans, widows, natives, uninsured, migrants – in their medical and dental needs and to help them to reach all levels of education."

Mexico provides health care for all who qualify through their program of social services. Some people, however, are not enrolled because they do not have the understanding, the credentials, or the work status. Women must have documented prenatal care in order be allowed to give birth in the hospital. Some women, especially from impoverished and rural areas, with limited transportation, cannot meet that criteria. Dr. Mendoza's services help overcome and bridge this and other barriers. The following is a transcript of Dr. Mendoza speaking to me in her interview in 2020, conducted all in English. She tells a compelling story.

Note: In this report, the term clinic refers to a medical care facility that does not offer surgery and does not have beds. In Mexico, it may be referred to as a dispensary.

I came to Juárez in the early 1980s. I was the first social doctor in Anapra. There were no government clinics in this area. I was the only source of care for years. That was before there was any infrastructure. We had to buy our water. Later on, missionaries started coming from other organizations to help out.

I have been a doctor for almost four decades. I graduated in 1979 with a medical degree from the University in Chihuahua City. At first, I was working in the rural mountain areas with the Tarahumara and Oaxaca Indians. Then I worked in hospitals in Chihuahua City. I learned that emergency room work is hard. I thought I would find something that was not so hard. I decided to move to Juárez to work in a recently built government hospital and ended up working in the emergency area. HA! This happened in the early 1980s.

In this work in the Juárez hospital, I was seeing so many vulnerable uninsured people, people who had no exposure to preventive medicine. And some were in the terminal stages of diseases that were treatable and preventable. In those days they did not have any separation between emergency room care and OB-GYN. I would see the young women; there were several like this. I asked, "Why are you here?"

"I am pregnant."

"How many weeks?"

"I don't know." Often, they had no idea.

"When is your due date?"

"I don't know. Nobody told me. My mother just told me it will hurt."

With all those stories, my eyes were wet with tears. Sometimes the girl would say, "I was feeling good but suddenly I broke into a fever and discharge came from my vagina. It smells bad."

Then I would find that the baby was dead. The girls often passed the due date. Sometimes the pelvis was not suitable for natural delivery. They had needed a C-section. They had no prenatal care! Everything was infected. Sometimes they had to have a hysterectomy and take the uterus and ovaries. And they were now with a dead baby. It resulted in surgical menopause. That gave me so much sadness.

Then I started thinking, while I am doing this sad work in the hospital, who is walking with these vulnerable people? I felt so much unrest. I was praying. Eventually, a nurse practitioner who was a missionary approached me. "I hear you have a heart for the vulnerable. I invite you to come to our mission." It was located near the Read-the-Bible Mountain [a hill in south Juárez where painted rocks are arranged to spell out in large letters *"La Biblia is la Verdad. Leela"* or "The Bible is the truth. Read it"].

I said, "I have a full-time job."

She said, "Just remember, when you want to serve Jesus, you can find vacation time or sick time and come see us."

One day I went to visit them. I found how a simple clinic was set up for medical and dental care. This was a Methodist missionary work. An American nurse practitioner was in charge. I started taking off work one day per week and going to this clinic. One day, I realized that was not enough. Eventually and gradually, I joined them and started practicing social medicine until this day.

When I was at Read-the-Bible Mountain Mission, carloads of people would come. They were illiterate. I started asking them questions. "Where are you working?"

They said they worked in the town. Even children were working. They said, "We don't go to school. We are rag-pickers at the garbage dump." That was about 1988.

In coordination with the director, we set up the first medical clinic at this large garbage dump in Juárez. Then I started inviting the people to come to the clinic. "Don't just come when you are desperate. There is preventive medicine. You should take advantage of that. We will show you how to stay away from the hospital. Hospitals are expensive."

In those days we did not have grants, and we were serving a lot of people. One family came to see me. "*Doctora*, we are coming to tell you we have found a family with leprosy."

"Well, invite them to come," I told them.

"No, they are ashamed."

I went to the dump and found them. It was not leprosy; it was just the scabies rash. They caught it from going through garbage. And they were scratching and scraping their skin with glass. In some cases, you could see the bone.

"Why have you not come to see me?"

"We heard there was a doctor, but it was not for us. We are rag-pickers."

"You are people. I want to work with you." We cured the scabies.

I learned that you can empower the people through health care and through education. I started encouraging children to continue in school. It was not so easy for them. "Well, my mother doesn't have money for shoes and uniform." Or, "The professor doesn't want me in school without the supplies." I started using my money and my husband's money to take care of these needs. We saw more children became interested in education. Soon, they were coming to my door asking for help to get their education. Some told us, "I want to go to school. I want to go to secondary school." And once they had their school degrees, some asked us, "Do you think people like us could go to university? Could we be accepted in university?"

I said, "Of course, if you pass the admission exam, I will get your tuition." Well, we had ten people who passed, and they came to me. They needed to be registered. I wasn't going to tell them no, but we didn't have the money.

I went to the authorities at the universities. "Listen, our students are excellent. They did well in school and passed the admission exam. But we don't have money. Is there any way you can give us payments and we can pay throughout the year?"

That official just smiled and reclined in his chair. "*Doctora* Mendoza, don't suffer. Your students are candidates for a scholarship. Scholarships are for students from underdeveloped areas. If they have excellent grades, if they pass the admission exam with a high score, if they are indigenous or handicapped, they can get free registration." I almost fainted! "Furthermore," he told me, "if they continue doing well the second semester, they will get the scholarship again." So, now, more than thirty students [from these vulnerable areas] have their university degrees through this.

Later on, an organization, Evangelical Lutheran Church of America, heard about my efforts so they started contributing. They sent money every semester for supplies.

Also, private individuals made some contributions directly to the students. In El Paso, there was a lady who won the lottery. She went to the dump to visit me. She said, "Hello, I am Ms. So and So. I just won the lottery and I want to join your effort." She helped support our students for about ten years.

My own father inspired me. My paternal side comes from mining; they were miners in the Tarahumara mountain area. My father only went to elementary school. My grandfather took him to the mine when he was just out of elementary school. My father told me he was malnourished, thin, and fragile at that time. The foreman said to my grandfather, "Why put your son in the hole? He is so young. No, no, no. We are not going to put him in the hole. He can be in charge of cleaning the grinder." My father said he would do that for eight hours every day.

He told me, "I would see the miners coming from home in clean clothes, laughing, joking, smiling, in a good mood. Then I would see them when they get out of the hole – black, covered in dust, barely crawling. I wondered, 'How strange. Why do only the brown men go down into the hole?'" The mine was owned by a company in New York. All the Americans working there were administrators. My father started realizing, "I know what the difference is. Education. I would like to get married in a place where my family has access to education."

After a few years, he rebelled, and told my grandfather, "I am not working any more in the mine. I am going to the city."

Grandfather said, "Not with my support."

So, he walked and caught rides with truckers, all the way to the city of Chihuahua. Once he was there, he struggled. But he educated himself as an electronic technician. He met my mother. They had their home. He told her, "I don't care if children go with bare feet and with patches. But they have to be educated."

He planted that seed for my love of knowledge. When you have those tools, you try to help your neighbor; to help the more vulnerable ones. God put in my path an ideal husband who shared my ideology. He volunteers as the maintenance man for several medical clinics across Juárez.

I am doing every year the same things. I work with mothers and then their grandchildren. They make the same mistakes. Pregnancies and the disadvantaged; it is endless work and I learned to take one day at a time. Some of the girls are without a caring partner, they have been raped, they don't know about birth control. Some do not have a blanket to take the baby home. They just wrap it in their jacket. We give them some supplies. Girls who have unwanted babies here – they just endure it.

The reason I do this is a very strong concern for empowering the vulnerable through education and health care.

Note: The Mexican government provides free birth control at the government clinics and hospitals. Dr. Mendoza's clinic is part of a non-profit Mexican Civil Association. They provide information about birth control.

Access to health care should be a human right, not a piece of merchandise to buy and sell to the privileged. We charge thirty pesos, less than two dollars for the introductory fee. If they do not have money, they are seen anyway. You know, once you start doing the work for the poor, the word gets around. Some react with solidarity.

Some become our divine providence. They come to the clinic. They donate supplies or medicine. Some doctors come to help us pro bono.

The director of the clinic at the dump passed away, and the new administrator had a different focus and raised prices for the services. I am not involved with that clinic now.

My husband still works, keeping the maintenance at the Read-the-Bible-Methodist Mission and another mission on the east side of Juárez. They are doing similar work like ours in Anapra. We share supplies and specialists. We also have a dental facility to restore teeth. Other dental care outreach can only cover cleaning and pulling the sick teeth. We try to save and fix as much as we can. We do some prostheses; for that we charge only the basic lab cost.

The dentist came several years ago. He came to volunteer for just two months. I don't want to remind him that he overstayed his time. HA!

What we do is health education, preventive medicine, and walk-in general practice. Some of my students have graduated as doctors. I was hoping they would come help in the clinic. One student wanted to be a specialist. I asked if he wanted to help me. He said, "You are too messy. Your waiting room is full of elderly women, babies, the wounded, the chronically ill." Well, that is the general practice here.

I had training in New Mexico and was licensed as a midwife, a lay midwife. During that training they instructed me in reflexology, pressure points, nutrition, homeopathic and herbal alternatives.

When the Indigenous people come, some do not trust

Western medicine. They say no to pills and chemicals. They only want herbs. I respect their culture. I examine them with their clothes on. I work with their beliefs. I help them with herbal cures. We follow the *Physicians' Desk Reference for Herbal Medicines*.

I do not do midwifery in Juárez. Midwifery is too high risk. Many people do not have good houses and good hygiene [for a home birth]. The Mexican government provides grant funds so that a woman can be in hospital for birth. I encourage the women to go to the government clinic or hospitals and to come to me also so they can get as much care as possible.

We live one day at a time. It is always a big load to keep our volunteers – medical assistants, dental assistants, physical therapists, doctors. Sometimes we do not have the resources they need. Divine providence comes to our door and compassionate and prominent specialists answer our cry for help as we advocate for these special communities.

SISTER ORGANIZATIONS

There are more formal and informal organizations in Anapra and Ciudad Juárez, organized by local women and providing life-saving support to the community. I mention two here. Junt@s Vamos was organized by an Anapra resident, Cristina Coronado, to provide support for women in Anapra and Ciudad Juárez who had cancer. Cancer treatment in the area was limited. The women had to travel to the state's capital, Chihuahua City, or even to Mexico City to get the care they needed. Junt@s Vamos organized fundraisers with U.S. friends and saved many women's lives. Mary Alice Scott provides fundraising venues for this cooperative.

In restaurants and homes in the border area, table covers in bold bright colors made of oilcloth are a common sight. Two nuns, Donna Kustusch and Eleanor Stech, created a center in a high poverty area in Ciudad Juárez, a cooperative of women to make these table covers and many other handcrafts. The center also provides tutoring for children, music lessons, a large organic garden, lunch, dental care, and spiritual education. The community center has been active and successful for more than twenty-five years.

~ 8 ~

SHELTER IN
THE JUNGLE

From my sixth-floor office at the university in El Paso I could see the streets and houses layered on the sandy hills of the western part of Ciudad Juárez. This was the early 2000s and maquiladora factories were rapidly locating there. That view made me question: How was this tremendous social change in Mexico impacting education? I received a research grant to help explore that question. The grant supported travel to schools and organizations across Mexico, in locations near large maquiladoras.

In the end, I found that support for local schools came mostly from the Mexican education programs, often enhanced with parent and community donations of time and money. I found only a few examples of support from the administrators of U.S. maquiladoras: a one-time gift such as painting the building, pouring a concrete slab, or providing materials or equipment. Ford Mexico (not a U.S. corporation) had built many schools across the country in low-income communities. I visited one of those schools south of Juárez and witnessed children working in a state-of-the art computer lab.

The heart and main story for this research project was

in Ciudad Juárez, which had the largest number of people working in these factories. That is when I started the visits and collaboration mentioned in the introduction with the elementary school in the Anapra area of Juárez.

I needed to know about other parts of Ciudad Juárez where maquiladora workers lived and what their schools were like. Juárez is a complex city. New migrants settle in unofficial neighborhoods. Maps can't keep up. I needed help.

A friend invited me to go with her one Sunday to visit a church in Juárez whose members included folks who worked in these factories. There I met Anay Palomeque Vazquez Carrillo, wife of a young preacher, Enrique. The family was living in one of the classrooms of the church complex with their baby daughter. In return for this living space, Enrique served as the church's youth minister.

Anay is pronounced: AN EYE. Her uncle gave her that name, in memory of his Maya girlfriend who was murdered when she was only seventeen. Carrillo is her husband's last name. Vazquez is her official and business name; however, it is also the name of the teacher who raped her mother when she was his thirteen-year-old student. Palomeque is the name of her beloved grandfather, and the name she prefers to use in unofficial settings.

That meeting and our friendship over the next ten years grew into a book, *Anay's Will to Learn: A Woman's Education in the Shadow of the Maquiladora*. Anay is a very gifted woman who has struggled through most every adversity that economic injustice can deliver to raise a happy family, get a college degree, and create a successful Mexican Civil Association which manages several projects supporting women's educational and economic success.

At that first meeting, I hired Anay to help me navigate Juárez and the maquiladora education communities. We spent several days each month visiting schools and factories, at first Anay, me, and baby Eva. As the family grew, I added baby carriers in the back seat and kept bags full of toys and books in the car. The family welcomed me into their humble house in a low-income area of Juárez.

Anay told me how she came to Juárez at age fifteen in a small van with seventeen other people to take a job in a maquiladora. The factories paid rather unethical men to visit poverty areas in the country and woo young folks to the border to fill the thousands of waiting jobs. The riders were promised good salaries, housing, and free education. None of that happened. The van broke down many times and was delayed by days. The riders slept on the roadside and ran short of food. Upon arrival, they were led into a warehouse and given a meal and a piece of cardboard for a bed. They started to work the next day.

She took me to her original home in Chiapas to meet family and friends. We visited the schools she attended and talked to her teachers.

Through the years, I often accompanied Anay and Enrique as they did mission work in Juárez and Chiapas. I recorded hundreds of pages of her memories and experiences.

That ended in 2010 when the gang violence in Juárez became severe. Anay's brother, Arturo, had borrowed money from a friend to pay the hospital fees for his wife who had recently had a baby. The friend used gang money for this loan. Arturo could not pay it back. The gangs asked him to work it off by killing opponents. He refused, knowing it would lead to his death. His friend invited him to a meeting downtown. Three cars were nearby. He stepped into the street and a shower of bullets from the cars took his life. Now, all his family members were in danger.

Anay, Enrique, the children, and many of their extended family fled to southern Chiapas, just north of the Guatemala border. This area of Mexico is renowned for natural beauty and is steeped in Maya history and culture. The family lived with Anay's grandmother on the outskirts of a town we will call Mixtla, in a very small village, or *ranchito*. Grandmother's home is surrounded by fruit trees, a vegetable garden, chickens and goats, and within walking distance through swampy land to the Pacific Ocean. The residents in the *ranchito* have been friends, relatives, and neighbors for generations. It is peaceful and safe. There is little money, but basic needs are met.

The downside is that severe floods surge through the area about every three years. Therefore, the homes are built simply. Weather reports warn them when the floods are coming. Everyone with a truck or car helps the others pack up the family and animals. They go to Mixtla and stay with other friends and relatives until the danger passes.

When the water recedes, they return to scrape the mud off the concrete slab, wash off the concrete sink and work area, reattach the hammock beds, replant the garden, and get back to life. They live in nature and with nature. Never easy, but this style of life endures for centuries.

LILY AND THE IMMIGRANTS

Anay and family were safe and surrounded by many relatives and friends. They put the children in school, and Enrique started mission and social programs in the surrounding villages. They became friends with the political leaders. Their mission work was much more than religious teaching. When they saw a problem, they helped solve it.

For example, they noticed that Guatemalan men would often walk through Mixtla on their way to the United States. They were sleeping on the streets. Anay and Enrique convinced the mayor to open an abandoned building so the travelers would have shelter for a few days. They found funds to feed the migrants. They taught the travelers about the realities of a trip north and their slim chance of finding a safe and prosperous life in the United States. Some of the migrants went home, others continued their journey.

While in Juárez, Anay had completed a degree in cosmetology. She saw the need for barbers and stylists in her hometown and the surrounding *ranchitos*. With help from a government labor-education program, she started a cosmetology school so the women could learn a skill and return to their rural communities to open a barber or beauty shop.

Anay also helped her students finish their junior high or high school degrees, tutoring them through a published program of books, quizzes, and exams to advance through the levels of the state-provided curriculum.

A petite sixteen-year-old, Lily, stopped by the beauty school one day. She had beautiful eyes, a severe deformity of her upper lip, and a cleft palate. Anay asked if she might be interested in the school. No, she said. She had no money. Anay invited her to attend and observe anytime she wanted, and she did.

Anay's husband did maintenance and improvements on the building. One evening, Enrique went to the convenience store on the main highway through town. Trucks often stop along this stretch for the night. He saw Lilly climbing up into the cab of a truck, stay a few minutes, leave, and go to another truck. He told Anay.

Anay asked Lily if she was selling sex to the truck drivers. "Yes, I am. I have three little brothers to feed. My father is an alcoholic living on the streets. My mother left years ago with another man. How can I get money? And the boys need food. So, I do this in the night when they are asleep. Then I buy the food for their breakfast and send them to school."

Anay's determination and sense of injustice flared. She asked Lily to come to the school every afternoon. She tutored her through the curriculum to get her high school degree. Lily was a quick learner and graduated. Then Anay located a business school in the area with a program in bookkeeping. Anay convinced the owner to admit Lily at a big discount. He did. Anay paid the rest in payments.

Now Lily is a successful bookkeeper working at a local bank. Enrique met Lily's father and invited him to help with his missionary church work. Papá now had some pride and guidance. He moved home with Lily and the boys and is drinking less and helping more.

A PLAN FOR EDUCATION

Enrique receives a small income from several church groups in Texas to support his missionary work in Chiapas. One year, his sponsors sent money to build a church building and home in Mixtla. Enrique hired several men. They poured a four-foot-deep cement foundation to support the building during the frequent earthquakes. And, thus far, the building has twice served as a refuge for others in the community when a quake shakes the earth. Enrique and his friends completed the shell of a two-story concrete block building that would be a small church on the bottom floor and a home on the top floor.

Then plans changed. Mexicans in the rural communities heard about Enrique's work. He preaches a very open message about supporting each other and building self-confidence and pride. And he uses his U.S. funding less for his family and more to meet a need – building a community center, a fence, or providing chickens. He was called more and more often to do mission work in these rural areas. Because of this work, they have many friends across rural Chiapas.

It can take hours, even days to reach a village, if the road is not washed out. And often, the vehicle will only go part way. You may walk the last few hours; sometimes a donkey is available.

Enrique discussed his new missions with his Texas funders. They agreed that the focus should change to working in the rural areas. Now, there was little need to build a central church building.

Meanwhile, Anay saw many young women in these rural communities with great academic potential. Most could attend high school near their village, although that required several hours of walking each day. When they graduated, their options narrowed.

In these rural areas, women traditionally have a set role: get married, have children, work in their *ranchito,* and help pick coffee beans, hoping to collect a few bags to sell at market to buy necessities.

Mexico is ahead of many developing nations in providing pre-university education options for its young people. Most everyone has access to elementary and middle school. High schools are not mandated; however, private secondary schools have been built recently throughout rural areas. Few are comprehensive. They are usually small, and they focus on an immediate need in the community – business, nursing, agriculture, or technical skills. Often, the curriculum is delivered by video with local tutors managing the face-to-face and workbook experiences.

This access to high-school education is relatively new in these rural areas. It has elevated the horizon for women, giving them a glance into a different future.

We traveled to Chiapas together in 2016. Anay showed me that partially finished building. "We need a place where these girls can stay. Then they can go to the university. The government will provide counselors. My Mexican Civil Association will give us tax breaks and the businesses are required to provide some donations. There are three small universities near here. The universities will give us scholarships. We just need to finish the building."

With help from Anay's family, the Guatemalan migrants, church friends, and funding from some U.S. family and friends, she finished the building. The city and universities provided support. Four years later, at the time of this writing, those partnerships with the universities are still in place. Five women graduated from their university in 2020 and twenty more are in the last years of high school or are successfully attending a university.

Anay's shelter was their lifeline to a future where they could use their talents to help their communities.

It has not been easy. Anay's gifted leadership style and obvious love and respect conquer many of the inevitable problems as they arise. Most of the girls have found jobs and work hard to help pay for their necessities while attending school. Some U.S. friends donate when they can. The local markets donate a portion of the needed food. Scholarships provide about half the tuition and fees. Transportation is costly as the girls must travel by taxi, and some campuses are up to forty miles away. Many women are studying to be nurses. Uniforms and medical tools are expensive.

Anay's friends and family in the community share pride in this work. The mayor of Mixtla hosted a grand opening when the shelter was finished with a party on the central plaza. Friends help with maintenance on the building, caring for the chickens and goats, giving the girls rides, and serving as mentors. More and more young women are asking to join the project.

Mexican Civil Associations, by law, are not connected to religious organizations. Anay keeps the church work separate from the Civil Association. However, some of her friends who provide financial support or volunteer at the shelter are also their church friends.

IN THE MAYA COFFEE LAND

One of Enrique's mission projects was in the Maya communities in northern Chiapas where coffee is the main economic crop. The coffee trees are scattered over the mountainsides, growing in harmony with other plants. The small farmers often work in cooperatives which provide insurance against nature's hail or floods.

Throughout Mexican history, wealthy colonialists or wealthy landlords enslaved the Maya to grow coffee in huge plantations, pick it, dry it, bag it, and carry it to market – enriching the pockets of the wealthy and robbing the land of its nutrients and the Maya families of their rights. Today, many Maya own their small farms. A culture of distrust for the Mexican government and wealthy capitalists remains.

Tito and his wife Noni, leaders of a small village of friends and relatives, have farmed the land for generations. The family extends to include Tito and Noni's children, Noni's sister and children, Tito's sister and children, a few children in the area whose parents were not able to care for them, and the little baby they found in the cornfield. Three main buildings of concrete block surround a large concrete patio where coffee beans are spread to dry. Other friends and relatives live in several smaller buildings along the dirt road running from the highway to the village center.

Enrique's mission work funded a small church building at the entrance of the village, built by the villagers. The church was the first thing we saw when we arrived by taxi. It was painted a bright blue and surrounded by three large trees. The door was open, and children were playing and running in and out. When the children saw Anay, they screamed and ran to her. She grabbed them up in giant hugs. They stared at the oversized white woman with her.

We walked to the center where Noni and her sister were raking the coffee beans to turn them for maximum exposure to the sunlight. Some of the women wore traditional Maya clothing and others were dressed in jeans, tee shirts, and flip flops. Fruit trees, vegetable plants, flowers, and coffee bushes dotted the landscape outside the village buildings. All the villagers speak their Maya language and most also speak Spanish.

A SHELTER FROM ABUSE

A few weeks before our visit, Tito had called Anay and asked her to come see his sister's daughters, Miriam, sixteen, and Kati, thirteen. "Something is wrong with them. They won't talk to me. They love you. Please come visit them."

When the girls arrived from their hour-long walk home from school, they hugged Anay, and greeted the old white lady politely. All the children went to the kitchen for their after-school meal of a soup, tortillas, and a lime drink. Anay stayed with the children, and I went back out to watch the coffee bean turning process.

A little later, Anay came out to the patio. Her lip was trembling when she told me. "I could tell by the look in their eyes that they were being abused. I asked them. It took a long time for them to tell me. But get this! Their teacher picks them up from school and takes them to a motel where he rapes them and then has other men pay to rape them! It has been going on for several weeks!"

Then Anay talked to Tito and explained what was going on. She asked him if we could invite the girls to come to the house in the city to stay and go to school. They would get counseling, a safe home, and school. He agreed. We went inside to ask the girls.

They were holding hands and sitting together on the edge of the bed with their eyes downcast. They had been crying. Anay explained their option of going to the shelter in Mixtla. That was the only time I saw light in their eyes and smiles on their faces. YES! They could start in a few weeks.

Anay made the arrangements with Tito. He would communicate with their mother who lived in another village where she had to work in another coffee field to pay for her children's school. Their father was in prison for murder. The story from the villagers is that he was falsely accused. The police were protecting a powerful man. The poor, indigenous man could take the blame; he would not be able to defend himself.

Around the world, approximately one in every three girls and one in every five boys suffer sexual abuse. The abuse is worse in areas of high poverty and isolation. In their book, *Half the Sky: Turning Oppression into Opportunity for Women Worldwide,* Nicholas Kristof and Sheryl WuDunn[6] detail many of the issues about global concerns for women's sexual health. "Behind the rapes

---

[6] Nicholas Kristoff and Sheryl WuDunn (2010). *Half the Sky: Turning Oppression into Opportunity for Women Worldwide.* Alfred Knopf: New York, pg. 67.

and other abuse heaped on women in much of the world, it's hard not to see something more sinister than just libido and prurient opportunism. Namely: sexism and misogyny."

Men also suffer in desperate societies, "but the brutality inflicted on women is particularly widespread, cruel, and lethal." The brutality is often embedded in the culture, and women are also the abusers, as we saw in Cuca's story.

When criminal gangs overwhelm a community, boys are stolen to be the soldiers and girls are stolen to be the sex slaves of the soldiers. Kristof and WuDunn document the atrocities of enslaving young girls in the sex trade in areas of developing countries where cultural practices deny women their human worth.

Anay and I were in Mixtla as the construction on the women's shelter was nearing the end. We stayed in the hotel near the highway, a comfortable and convenient place where businessmen and some businesswomen stay – mostly for agricultural and technology-communication related meetings. Walking up the stairway, we met a girl who looked to be about fourteen. She was dressed as if for church, her hair done up, tasteful makeup, and a new dress. She greeted us with a big smile. We noticed that she sat alone at one of the tables in the hotel's restaurant. We left to go to the shelter to work.

When we came back that evening, the hotel's owner, a friend of Anay's, told her that an older man met the girl for lunch. They left together. About an hour later, the girl returned, disheveled and crying – obviously raped. "What can I do?" asked Anay's friend with tears in her eyes. "This happens often. The rich businessman pays the parents for their daughter!"

One day, when Enrique was working in a rural community, one of the men, a member of his church, asked Enrique, "Can I buy Eva [their thirteen-year-old daughter at that time] and then you and I can be family." The man was married. Eva would be his extra.

Enrique understood that this was a cultural tradition, and although extremely repulsive, it would have to be handled gently. "Oh, you see I am married to Anay," he told the man. "I will have only one woman because I love her. Our daughter is much too young. She will go to school because we want a good life for her. Your children should go to school too." Anay and Enrique model this strong mission of education for girls. (Eva is now at a university in the United States on a scholarship in pre-med.)

SEX ABUSE PREVENTION CURRICULUM

Kristof and WuDunn's book also provides compelling evidence that women's education is the single most valuable resource available to improve women's position in society. They cite studies showing that women's education reduces sexual abuse, and that empowering women raises the overall economy and improves community health and well-being.

I was making plans to find the teacher who raped Miriam and Kati. Visions of the torture I would inflict on him lulled me to sleep at night.

"That is not the answer," Anay told me. "The Mexican government organizations, yes, even the schools, are obligated to collaborate with Mexican Civil Associations. We need a curriculum for sexual abuse, and the schools will have to teach it. Miriam and Kati can go with us to that school and they will teach our curriculum to all the teachers. That teacher will have to do what they say!"

We went to rape crisis centers and shelters on the U.S. side. They shared valuable resources with us. They showed us their facilities and told us how they present their education programs in the schools. They insisted that a successful education program must include a strong treatment program for victims. The staff who present the lessons in the school told us that, as they are teaching the basic definition of sexual abuse, in most classrooms they can tell by the expression on a child's face that he or she has probably suffered some form of abuse. They are then able to work with teachers, school counselors, police officers, lawyers, social workers, psychologists, families, and the courts to identify the abuse and to treat the child.

Anay explained. "In our schools, if we teach a lesson like that, too many children will show us they have been abused. We have only a little help. Every city has an organization for children and families with counselors. But not enough. We must start with prevention. We can do the treatment when we can, but there is not enough help to treat all who need it."

We found research and programs about what works best for prevention of sexual abuse. We found Mexican organizations and some Mexican laws that are designed to reduce sexual abuse (although in many areas those laws are not enforced). With help from U.S. and Mexican organizations and professionals who deal with sexual abuse, a curriculum for sexual abuse prevention emerged. The major themes are:

- History and facts of sexual violence.

- How to prevent sexual abuse and rape by someone you know.

- Creating a Declaration of Student Rights for Sexual Safety in the schools.

- The Second Rape, exposing the sad fact that rape most often leads to further abuse through humiliation, punishment, accusations, and siding with the abuser.

- Uniting against sexual violence.

- Pregnancy prevention

Schools and government organizations in and around her home communities have supported Anay in this effort. They reviewed the materials, often modifying them to meet their cultural context and their students' cognitive and development levels. They piloted them in community centers, schools of nursing, and all elementary and middle schools in Mixtla. A doctor in a Zapotec community and a teacher in a Maya community translated the materials into the native languages so they can use it with their people. Enrique shares the curriculum as part of his mission work. Response has been enthusiastic and some friends are also translating the materials to other Maya dialects.

The curriculum remains dynamic and is modified continually to meet the needs of the community. At this point, the curriculum is spreading by word of mouth. Publication, distribution, and training are ongoing.

WHAT THE TAXI DRIVER SAW

As we were traveling around Chiapas, we hired a taxi for the day to get us to our meetings. The driver overheard some of our conversation and told us, "You are doing important work. I drive in [*name withheld*] town. It is near a military base. You can often see little girls, maybe twelve years old. They are on the street, drunk or with a bottle of beer, and pregnant. Can you go there please?"

Anay's Civil Association is named Seeds of Love, *Granos de Amor*. The main office is located in Ciudad Juárez. The webpage is GRANOSDEAMOR.com. Many lives have been improved through her efforts. Yet the task ahead is urgent and unending. One day we will respond to the taxi driver's request.

ALTRUISM BORN OF SUFFERING

Knowing the women in this book makes it very hard to villainize them, hard to fear them, hard to see them as anything other than friends worthy of our admiration. They accomplish acts of goodness despite the difficulties they have endured and continue to endure. This phenomenon of reclaiming your own dignity after suffering violence to become caring and helpful has a name – Altruism Born of Suffering. Ervin Staub,[7] a psychiatrist and expert on Rwanda's forgiveness and

---

[7] Ervin Staub and Johanna Vollhardt. Altruism Born of Suffering: The Roots of Caring and Helping After Victimizing and Other Trauma. (2008). *The American Psychological Association*. Vol. 78, no. 3. 267-80.

reconciliation, coined the term and is the primary author of many studies on Altruism Born of Suffering.

Some people who are victims of severe violence, discrimination, or persecution turn to violence and self-harm. Yet others turn to caring, loving altruism. Staub states that he has little information that can predict which way the abused individual will turn.

Like Anay and Inéz, many abused women have an increased awareness of suffering and identify with other victims. They feel a greater sense of responsibility to prevent more suffering. They focus beyond the self. The Sisters at Santo Niño and the directors at Las Hormigas center learned through working with the women that providing a venue where the women have a role as a caring teacher, counselor, or caregiver led them to take important steps to healing and to focus beyond the self.

The last woman we meet in these stories is Grecia. Anay found her and her three children in downtown Ciudad Juárez, wondering, homeless, and confused. This was during the "Build-That-Wall" era in the Trump administration. Her journey fleeing danger in Guatemala and hoping to cross into the United States is not uncommon. It provides a little more insight into the recent immigrant experience.

~ 9 ~

GRECIA'S JOURNEY

Early in the spring of 2020, in a park in Ciudad Juárez, Anay met a family who had recently arrived from Guatemala. They were homeless and desperate, so Anay let them stay in her vacant house in southern Juárez. Grecia and her children (16, 15, and 11) arrived on May 1, 2019, a trip of more than 2,000 miles. She formally asked for asylum at the border between El Paso and Ciudad Juárez and received her paperwork on January 25, 2020. Her *Hearing in Removal Proceedings in Immigration Court* in El Paso was scheduled for June, although all proceedings were cancelled. She too lived in an unstable and certain zone where options for the future become more and more austere. This is her story as she told it.

LIFE IN GUATEMALA

I will start at the beginning. My life was very difficult. I was abused by my mother. She never called me "dear." One time I was with my father, and my mother said, "You are sleeping with him!" She yelled that. It hurt me so much. I was just eleven years old. "NO! He is my papá."

She was always punishing me and saying, "Get out of here."

To get away, I married a person who turned out to be very bad. I had three children with him. But he changed. He became abusive, saying horrible things and hitting me. He found a girlfriend. She was MS-13, a very bad gang. All her family is part of that gang. Manuel came out full of tattoos. He came home some days, but only to attack me.

One day, when my daughter was just fourteen, I received a call from the principal. "Grecia, did you send the father to pick up your daughter? He is outside. She is crying. Come to get your daughter." I hurried, taking a taxi to the school.

It was exactly like they told me. They were in the car, him and that girl, saying to my daughter, "Just come with us. You will like it. You will get a lot of money to buy things."

Finally, she told them, "Let me go get the books I need for my homework." But really, she went inside to the principal. That is when they called me.

Then he was always calling my daughter. He wanted to make her be part of the gang. Make her sell drugs at her school! And she is so pretty. [She wiped her eyes and shook her head.] So, we went to [the town where her parents live]. But he would still come to see us and scare the kids, say awful things to me.

We didn't have food, so I called him. "I don't have money. Give us money. Your kids need food."

He said, "Yes, meet me tomorrow in the plaza, and I will give you a lot. And come alone. Promise you will come alone."

I said, "Yes." But the kids heard that. And they told me not to go, and they came with me. He came with his lover. The kids were hiding behind a tree.

"Is it money you want?" he said.

"Yes."

"Here is your money." He pulled out a gun!

My kids saw that and came running. They grabbed him. "No, Papá. No, Papá."

"Why did you bring the kids? I told you to come alone." I told him that they heard the call. He was mad. He got in the car with his girlfriend, and they drove away. He gave us no money.

We went home, we were all crying so much. I had to go to the neighbors begging for food. What was I going to do? I couldn't work. In Guatemala, if you are more than forty years old there is no work. I am forty-two. I looked and looked for work. I could not find any.

I found a man who sold cocaine. "You can work for me. If you help me, I will help you." We needed so much, but I would not do that.

I sold the stove, the refrigerator, beds, and almost all my things. We got [she stopped to calculate the exchange] about two thousand pesos [$100 U.S.]. I told my children, "We are going with this money. I don't know where, but we are going."

IN TABASCO

I had a friend on Facebook, Rosie, who lives in Tabasco. We talked a lot through Facebook. I told her about the bad things that had been going on. She said, "I am a single mother too. Come here. I have a bakery. You can work here with me. Come." She told me how to get there. First, we went to Hidalgo in Guatemala where it is easy to cross into Mexico. Then we were in a *combi* [a community van transport]. And we had to cross a river on a raft. The kids were scared of that raft and cried. But we were in Mexico, and we went on a bus to Tuxtla. There, [the Mexican border patrol officers] came on the bus. I was so scared. One of the older officers asked me where I was going. "To Tabasco to see a cousin." He didn't say anything else. He let us go.

Rosie picked us up at the bus station. She was nice until we got to her house. Then she said, "I am your husband's lover on Facebook." She showed me the pictures he sent her and love notes they sent each other! "You will stay here because you don't have any place to go. You can sleep here in my house and cook for me and watch my kids."

It was hot. My home in Guatemala is cool in the mountains. She gave us each one sheet, and we slept on the floor. I was not afraid of her because she was alone, too, with three kids.

She got up and went to work from six to six, and we stayed with her kids and did all the housework and cooking. Her kids got three meals every day, but we only got two small meals. She had another boyfriend who was a truck driver. One day she left on a trip with him and left some money for her kids and told me to watch them. I gave her kids the money, and we left. We had been with her twenty-five days. We got no pay. We were her slaves!

Then I was in the park in Tabasco. A woman came up to me. "You are a migrant. Your face tells me everything." I told her what had been happening and that I was a slave with Rosie. "Oh, my husband drives a bus, and it goes to Monterrey in two days. If you want to go to Monterrey, he can get you there in two days." I didn't know where Monterrey was.

We went to her house and the husband said, "It is twelve hundred pesos [$60 U.S.]. But don't worry, I'll take you and the three kids on my bus."

IN MONTERREY

When we arrived in Monterrey at the bus terminal, a man – we thought he was nice – invited us to his house. But he locked us in a room. I told him that my daughter was sick, and he left. We escaped to a migrant shelter.

There we met two young men from El Salvador. They had lived undocumented in the U.S., but they got sent back. They were going to cross again with a *coyote*. They told me that it was too dangerous to cross like that with my kids. They told me that I could ask for asylum at the border. I didn't know what that was. The social worker at the migrant center told me about asking for asylum. She told me, "You need to go to Juárez, but it is very far."

The young men told me, "In the night, we will go on the train. You can come with us and we will show you how." [These brave travelers run alongside a slow-moving train and jump for a handhold. Then they climb up and travel on top of the train.]

I was afraid to trust them, but we went with them and spent the night beside the tracks. In the morning, the young men brought food to my kids.

The train was going so fast. My kids could not get on with it going that fast. Another train was coming. I thought, "What am I going to do? I know. I'll get pregnant." I took one of the sweaters from my backpack and rolled it up and put it under my shirt. I put some other things over it. When the train came, I was waving, pointing to my stomach, begging for a ride. The driver nodded yes and stopped the train!

That man got down and said, "Where are you going?"

"Torreon."

"How many months are you?"

"Eight months."

"Here, you and your kids can get in this car." It was a boxcar with pallets on the floor. I think it was where the workers were sleeping. "You will be okay here. When we get to Torreon, we will tell you."

We arrived early in the morning and found a place to stay under some trees.

A woman came out. She was a big woman with a grey uniform for her work. She came close to me. "You are migrants? I have been looking for you." She made a shriek. "You are exactly like in my dream. Even with your three children. I am supposed to help you."

"Are you sure?" I asked her.

"Yes, I am Angela. Come to my house. I don't have a husband, and my only son died when he was only eight months. Because of this I look for people who are in need. I will take you to my big house. I have many migrants in my house. They all call me Madre Angela. I work seven to four in the factory. There is food for you in the refrigerator. Where are you going?"

"To Juárez to ask asylum for my kids."

"How?

"On the train."

"No! That is very dangerous. There are many drug

gangs on the train. I do not want you to go like that. Here is what we will do. Give me two days to work. Then I can buy tickets for you. I love your kids and I don't want them on the train."

She left us there. Others arrived with the same problems, like us, but no one came with small children. We stayed for four days. She was so lovely. Then she took us to the center of town and bought the tickets.

"Grecia, here is food for your kids. You will travel all night." She hugged us.

La Migra [Mexican border patrol] was checking when we got on the bus. "You are migrants?"

I was angry now. "Yes, from Guatemala. If you want to make me go back, just kill me. I will not return to Guatemala! You do not know what I have suffered there. If you want to send us back, I prefer you just kill us now. Go ahead."

He said, "Get on the bus."

At the Chihuahua border, again *La Migra* got on the bus. I told the kids to sleep. Sleep. We acted asleep. The man did like this, [she tapped her shoulder] "Senora. Senora." He asked another migrant, "Where are you going?" Then he did it again, but I just stayed with eyes closed. He walked away. At seven-thirty in the morning on the first day of May, we got to the Juárez bus terminal.

IN CIUDAD JUÁREZ

When we arrived in Ciudad Juárez, we walked to a park. This man, Arturo, came up to me. He said that the police would arrest us if they found us. "Come with me. You will be safe at my house."

When we got there, it was near Parque Borunda in an old house, and there were forty-two migrants in the room. All were men! He said for us to go in.

"No! Not with my children."

"Then you will have to go to the street." Well, we went in there. They were all staring at my daughter. He said, "There is the food. You can cook for all of us." So, I did cook a lot of food. Then they started drinking. I went to a corner and put the kids on the floor to sleep. But I stayed sitting up. I was getting nervous. I got the kids and we left there.

A car passed by. A woman asked if we needed help. "Get in. You can trust us. We are preachers." They let us stay in their house for two days. Then they said, "I know a woman who makes burritos. You can stay with her and help with her work. The woman's son goes to our church."

We stayed three months in her house. I got up a four in the morning to make burritos for her son to sell in the streets. We got one egg, one tortilla, frijoles, and water in the morning and a *nopal* [part of a cactus, common food in Mexico] and salsa with frijoles in the afternoon. Just water to drink. We did all the cooking, washing dishes, cleaning the house, washing clothes, everything. There were lots of dogs and cats. It was dirty. We had just one bed. They said they would pay me [$15 U.S.], but every week they said, "No, you and your kids ate too much food."

I told her I was going to look for work. She said, "No, it is dangerous. You need to stay here. You cannot leave because there are no buses and *La Migra* is all around." So, I did not leave.

Then I went outside once and it was not true. There were buses passing all around. I met a man, Antonio, who had a little food stand in [a nearby neighborhood]. "Come and work here and I'll pay you." So, we left that lady's house. Well, Antonio paid a little, but he never paid what I needed. He had a little room. We stayed a month there.

One day, we were in the park. That is when I met Anay. She talked to my daughter. I was so afraid of her. She said, "No, don't worry. There is a house where you can live."

Now we are safe. But my daughter is depressed. She missed her *quinceañera* [Latin-American coming out party for girls]. She doesn't want to bathe or do anything. She can't sleep. My older son is so quiet. He is always hugging me. "Don't worry, Mamá. I am here with you." He is too young.

While I was interviewing Grecia, Anay took the kids shopping for new shoes and a cake. When they returned, we had a pretend *quinceañera* party for Nina. She was giggling and dancing when they came in with her cake.

In June 2021, Grecia and the children were allowed to enter the United States to seek asylum. Their brothers and sisters in the Mormon church gave them home and sponsorship in Salt Lake City, Utah.

~ 10 ~

SEEKERS OF A
STABLE SKY

Many of the individuals in these stories are or have been immigrants in the United States. Some with legal status, some without. Young Minerva supported her family by slipping over the border to beg or work small jobs. Inéz fled north in fear of her son's safety. Cuca's son crossed illegally and found a job in Oklahoma. He sends money when he can. Sara immigrated in reverse. She now lives full time in Anapra, leaving her home in southern New Mexico. The Mexican government awarded Anay a scholarship to study international business anywhere she wanted. She chose the University of Texas at El Paso and is now in the United States on a student visa. Grecia received permission to cross. While she was waiting, she finished an online graduate degree in business.

I recently had a serious health problem. The four doctors who cured me were immigrants from Mexico, Honduras, India, and Pakistan.

In communities where there are many immigrants, there is less crime, and immigrants pay billions of dollars in U.S. taxes. The great majority of residents in El Paso, Texas, are first- and second-generation immigrants from

Mexico. El Paso consistently makes it to the top of lists of safest cities in the United States. Businesses across the United States are desperate for the inexpensive labor that immigrants provide.

In the early 2000s, border apprehensions were often over one million per year. Those large numbers were managed through a system of laws and regulations designed with some attempt at justice (not always implemented justly) within the U.S. and international legal immigration systems. Unrest in El Salvador, Guatemala, Honduras, Cuba, and conflict in the Middle East added to the numbers of desperate people attempting to cross legally and illegally. Their attempts to get to a safe place are filled with danger. The trip itself is dangerous, and it is very likely they will be robbed, raped, kidnapped, killed, or held for ransom until their family at home or in the United States pays a large fee.

This immigrant experience, in Ciudad Juárez, during the Trump presidency, is a significant historic event. It could easily get lost in the vast, confusing, politically raw timeline. In this chapter, we document pieces of that border experience from reliable news sources and from the experiences of friends and organizations who were directly involved in the immigrant story.

In many developing countries, long plagued with political and economic struggles, social unrest has increased; drug and gang violence threaten thousands of innocent citizens; and political and economic unrest upset vestiges of stability. We heard consistent stories documenting the asylum-seeking parent's fear, like Grecia, that their child was targeted by drug gangs. The majority of these individuals have families and friends in the United

States who will host them and provide for their needs while they go through the immigration or asylum legal processes.

All too often, unethical human traffickers lead the trek to the north, robbing and abusing their travelers along the way. The smugglers delude their victims and woo them with promises of crossing, showing bogus video testimonials of people who came to the United States and claim they live the good life. The traveler pays large sums of money to the smuggler. Once they arrive at the border, they are extorted for more money and often forced to carry drugs across. Drug cartels and human smugglers collaborate in the abuses, kidnappings, robberies, and sometimes death. However, the smugglers still find willing people among those who are blinded by that hope for a better life.

Many seekers are misinformed about the United States immigration and asylum regulations; as they told reporters, they brought their families to the border because they heard that families with children were allowed to enter the United States. Anay's cousin called her one day. "We are coming to the United States to stay with you. This man said he will take us to the border, and we can cross because you live there." A few months later, another friend called her with the same request. Anay had to crush their hopes with the reality that they were being victimized.

There are, of course, many people carrying illegal drugs across the border to fill the very lucrative U.S. demand. Smuggling contraband over the U.S. borders may never go away. That problem is particularly difficult to deal with, but efforts to slow the flow might address the supply *and* the demand side.

Misinformation, rumors, crime, fear, and desperation fuel the flow of people seeking entrance in the United States. The continental truth, however, that cannot be ignored is that wealth in the United States is blaringly greater than in Latin American countries, and that most U.S. residents live in much safer conditions than residents of the two-thirds world. That is a powerful magnet for families living in poverty – an enormous, frosted cupcake flaunting itself.

THE U.S. IMMIGRATION SYSTEM IN 2019–2020

As of March 2019, the El Paso border stations were processing 500–600 individuals each day.[8] A backlog of those new arrivals entering the immigration process had built up. Agents fenced off an area under the border bridge and some 3,500 were held there for days.

The migrants were jostled among several agencies involved in the apprehension, processing, detention, deportation, and/or the Return to Mexico programs. The overarching agencies were the U.S. Department of Homeland Security and the Department of Justice. The enforcing agencies were U.S. Customs and Border Protection (CBP), Immigration and Customs Enforcement (ICE), U.S. Citizenship and Immigration Services, the

---

[8] United States Border Patrol Total Illegal Alien Apprehensions by Fiscal Year (Oct. 1st through Sept. 30th). Retrieved August 2, 2020, from https://www.cbp.gov/sites/default/files/assets/documents/2019 -Mar/BP%20Total%20Apps,%20Mexico,%20OTM%20FY2000-FY 2018%20REV.pdf

Office of Refugee Resettlement (ORR), the U.S. Marshals Service, and local law enforcement.

One significant change in this immigration policing process beginning in 2018 – something seldom done in previous administrations – was the separation of young children from their parents; sending them to detention centers not designated for little children, all alone, in cages, or scattered into foster homes across the nation; some 14,000 in 2019. Documentation of these children and their rightful parents was inadequate, and, at the time of this writing, more than 600 families still had not found their children. Confusion was rampant. For example, a twelve-year-old boy who fled drug gangs was deported, alone, back to Guatemala while his mother was waiting for him in the United States.[9, 10]

In the 2019 confusion, border agencies (although the agencies had successfully managed much greater numbers in past years) were overwhelmed. Policies and approaches were chaotic. Some officials tried holding the immigrant-seekers in the cages at the border. Others sent them to privately-owned jail-like detention centers. Tent cities were set up. Some were bused to U.S. border cities and released at a bus stop or in the city's downtown, basically

---

[9] Nomann Merchant, Seeking Refuge in the US, Children Fleeing Danger Are Expelled. Washington Times, August 6, 2020, Retrieved August 19, 2020, from https://www.washingtontimes.com/news/2020/aug/6/seeking-refuge-in-us-children-fleeing-danger-are-e/

[10] Jacob Soboroff, Despite Judge's Order Migrant Children Remain Detained Amid Covid. July 23, 2020. NBC News. Retrieved July 24, 2020, from https://www.nbcnews.com/politics/immigration/despite-judge-s-order-migrant-children-remain-detained-amid-covid-n1234705

abandoned with little more than the clothes they had been wearing for weeks.

In response to this action of releasing the immigrants in border cities, social organizations in the El Paso / southern New Mexico regions – most were part of religious groups – built support structures in record time and provided temporary housing, showers, and food. I witnessed the efforts of the Catholic-sponsored Annunciation House in El Paso and the Lutheran-sponsored Border Servants Corps in Las Cruces. At that time, they collaborated with the National Guard to locate the families to one of these welcoming shelters, mostly in church buildings in communities along the border. The immigrants all had family or friends who would give them a home in the United States. The volunteers worked with each family to contact their hosts, and the hosts paid for and arranged for someone to pick them up, or a bus ticket, and sometimes an airplane ticket.

Within a few days, these organizations had gathered donations of food, clean clothes, some books, and games for children on their journey. I helped a little. The families were assigned a number and then met us in the clothing room. I helped them find shoes and socks. After these many days in the hot desert with no shower, they all had smelly feet. They were embarrassed. I learned the Spanish phrases that helped them laugh and understand that it was unavoidable. Then they took their clean clothes to the shower room and came back with shiny hair to thank us. Some left immediately and some waited a day or two for their transportation.

After a few months, the Trump administration set up

a "cure for the immigrant problem" that stretched and broke immigration laws and human rights codes so that no one seeking asylum at the southern border would be allowed to enter or stay in the United States while their petition was being processed. They were quickly and carelessly sent back across the border. The new practice was *mis*named Migrant Protection Protocols (MPP), commonly called "Remain in Mexico."

The numbers indicate that those efforts had little permanent effect. Nicole Narea's report[11] in Vox covers several studies that show that detention and deportation do little to prevent people in difficult situations from trying to enter the United States. The enemy you know is worse than the enemy you don't know.

HOW DID "REMAIN IN MEXICO" WORK?

In June 2019, President Trump forced the Mexican government to comply with this policy. The following is quoted from Vandana Rambaran's June 7, 2019, report on Fox News.[12]

---

[11] Nicole Narea, June 3, 2021. The false promises of more immigration enforcement: Harsh detention and deportation policies haven't deterred migrants. Vox.com. Retrieved June 23, 2021, from https://www.vox.com/policy-and-politics/22451177/biden-border-immigration-enforcement-detention-deportation

[12] Vandana Rambaran, June 7, 2019. US Makes Deal with Mexico on Tariffs, Immigration, Trump Announces. Retrieved August 3, 2020, from https://www.foxnews.com/politics/us-makes-deal-with-mexico-on-tariffs-immigration-trump-announces

The deal, announced by President Trump via tweet on Friday night, is said to include plans to return migrants seeking asylum to Mexico, where they will remain until their claims can be processed.

"I am pleased to inform you that The United States of America has reached a signed agreement with Mexico. The Tariffs scheduled to be implemented by the U.S. on Monday, against Mexico, are hereby indefinitely suspended. Mexico, in turn, has agreed to take strong measures to...stem the tide of Migration through Mexico, and to our Southern Border. This is being done to greatly reduce, or eliminate, Illegal Immigration coming from Mexico and into the United States. Details of the agreement will be released shortly by the State Department. Thank you!"

Trump was proposing a 5 percent tariff on Mexican goods, which would increase up to 25 percent every month, potentially harming American consumers and manufacturers who purchased $378 billion worth of Mexican imports in 2018.

The Fox report did not mention how the tariff would harm the Mexican consumers and manufacturers.

The Department of Homeland Security claimed that "Remain in Mexico" was more humanitarian, ensured safety of migrants, and ensured access to attorneys. We have found almost no evidence that supports those claims. By most accounts, "Remain in Mexico" was illegal – a violation of several national and international immigration and refugee laws.[13]

As the migrants were abandoned, they were subject to abuse from criminal elements. Access to legal help and legal rights was greatly restricted. Bilingual immigration lawyers did exist, but very few would cross into Juárez to try to present one of thousands of cases to a court that was not accessible and whose judges had been ordered to deny petitions and rewarded for doing so.

There were reports of corruption and crime within the U.S. border agencies. In August 2020, three women held in an El Paso detention center claimed they suffered repeated sexual abuse. Border Patrol agents had criminal arrests at rates higher than other law enforcement agents.

In 2019, 9,500 Border Patrol agents, including a supervisor in El Paso, were on a secret Facebook group filled with racist, indecent, and lurid content. One doctor was accused of performing hysterectomies and other invasive surgeries on women in the detention centers without their knowledge or consent.[14, 15]

---

[13] U.S. Department of Homeland Security, Migrant Protection Protocols. Retrieved August 2, 2020, from https://www.dhs.gov/news/2019/01/24/migrant-protection-protocols

[14] Lomi Kriel. ICE Guards "Systematically" Sexually Assault Detainees in an El Paso Detention Center, Lawyers Say. ProPublica, August 14, 2020. Retrieved August 15, 2020, from https://www.propublica.org/article/ice-guards-systematically-sexually-assault-detainees-in-an-el-paso-detention-center-lawyers-say

[15] A.C. Thompson, Inside the Secret Border Patrol Facebook Group Where Agents Joke about Migrant Deaths and Post Sexist Memes. ProPublica. Retrieved August 2, 2020, from https://www.propublica.org/article/secret-border-patrol-facebook-group-agents-joke-about-migrant-deaths-post-sexist-memes

During that time, "Remain in Mexico" ejected some 300,000 of these displaced asylum seekers and migrants back over the border into Mexican border towns – with no support, no supplies, and only a few pages of vague information. The United States provided them with nothing; and the United States gave Mexico nothing for hosting them.

To be more efficient, border agents along the border sent their asylum seekers to the larger border cities for processing. Therefore, hundreds of thousands were processed at the El Paso-Ciudad Juárez border – 851,508 of the 859,501 total apprehensions in 2019.[16]

WHERE WERE THESE THOUSANDS OF ASYLUM SEEKERS TO GO?

These individuals and families were dropped off across the bridge on the Mexican side where they were to "wait" for their number to be called – waiting in a hopeless unknown. Early in the fall of 2019, many who entered Ciudad Juárez just sat down on the sidewalk that was a few feet from the bridge in downtown and stayed. Others found churches or friends to help. Some returned home.

Non-profit groups and individuals on both sides of the border responded. Red Cross Mexico provided health

---

[16] United States Border Patrol. Total Illegal Apprehensions By Fiscal Year (Oct. 1st through Sept. 30th). Retrieved August 2, 2020, from https://www.cbp.gov/sites/default/files/assets/documents/2020-Jan/ U.S.%20Border%20Patrol%20Total%20Monthly%20Family%20U nit%20Apprehensions%20by%20Sector%20%28FY%202013%20- %20FY%202019%29_0.pdf

screenings. Volunteers with Migrant Support Network, Border Servant Corp, and other humanitarian organizations provided sandwiches, water, foam mats, blankets, and other basics. For several months, U.S. volunteers walked across that bridge carrying food and supplies in their rolling luggage. As the weather got colder, the non-profit groups found tents for the migrants. An Episcopalian minister from Boston started a street school.

One day in the fall, military officials in Juárez sent bulldozers to clear the sidewalks. The people scattered with their most vital possessions. The rest of the possessions were scooped up and discarded.

Human rights organizations, churches, and border residents on both sides of the border worked hard to find the migrants and help ease the difficulties inflicted on them. For a few months, many migrants were in churches and non-profit centers; however, as the Covid-19 infection rates rose, many of those locations were forced to close. The Chihuahua state government operates a migrant transition facility which, with the surge of people expelled to Juárez, was overwhelmed. The director had been pleading for help for months.

The Mexican government responded and sent millions of pesos to provide shelter and some level of basic care for the thousands of abandoned people. Late in 2019, in Ciudad Juárez, a vacant factory was converted into the new migrant center. It started with 12,000 and thousands more were waiting in the system.[17]

---

[17] Julian Resendiz. New Migrant Shelter Opens in Juárez. *The Border Report.* August 1, 2019. Retrieved June 22, 2020, from https://www.ktsm.com/news/border-report/new-migrant-shelter-opens-in-Ju%C3%A1rez-2/

This was the first Mexican government-sponsored shelter. There were plans to establish similar shelters in other Mexican border cities which were also receiving many "Return to Mexico" migrants. The Juárez shelter was set up with separate sleeping facilities, accommodations for families, restrooms, and a cafeteria. It was not able to provide shelter for unaccompanied children; a special center for children was opened in downtown Juárez.

The Mexican government also provided some extent of health care and education. Some adult migrants applied for work permits. If approved, the migrant could look for work in Juárez, and, if lucky, eventually have resources for food and housing and leave the shelter. Hope Border Institute and the Catholic Diocese of El Paso were among the groups who assisted in providing support to the migrants in the factory-turned-shelter. The non-profit organization *Seguimos Adelante* (We Walk On) took food into Ciudad Juárez to the homes and centers where asylum seekers were waiting.

Chihuahua Labor Undersecretary Horacio Duarte stated that the expense the Mexican government would incur in building shelters is far less than what Trump's tariffs would have cost Mexico.[18]

The Border Servant Corps identified at least fifteen additional, mostly informal centers that were hosting asylum seekers in Ciudad Juárez in 2020.

---

[18] Julian Aguilar. August 2, 2019. *The Texas Tribune*, Pulitzer Center. As El Paso Closes Emergency Migrant Shelters, Mexico Scrambles to Add Space on the Border. Retrieved August 2, 2020, from https://pulitzercenter.org/reporting/el-paso-closes-emergency-migrant-shelters-mexico-scrambles-add-space-border

Matamoros, near the mouth of the Rio Grande, was also host to many of these asylum seekers; stranded folks trying to survive while living in a tent city. They were supported by a collective of U.S. organizations in Brownsville, Texas, named Dignity Village. The tent city had about 600 in late 2020 with 2,500 at its peak. They lived with flooding, mud, rain, heat, mosquitos, and an unpredictable river, waiting for that dizzying hope for a chance to cross legally.

Also in response to the U.S. demands, the Mexican military were forced to increase policing on their southern border with Guatemala. Central Americans now faced a new and serious barrier in Mexico as they tried to flee from the danger in their homeland. Trump withheld aid to Central America until they complied with his wishes and strengthened their own border immigration policing. Record breaking and devastating hurricanes in 2020 increased Central Americans' desperation to travel north to seek a safe home.

These one-sided laws, in their 'un' justice, are weapons against people who are desperate and begging for help. Humanity, thus, is reserved for the wealthy few on the planet. Sonia Shah,[19] a scientist who studies migration in many forms, explains that, throughout human and ecological history, migration most often results in immigrants quickly assimilating, integrating, and adapting.

---

[19] Sonia Shah (2020). *The Next Great Migration: The Beauty and Terror of Life on the Move.* Bloomsbury: New York.

WHAT ARE DETENTION CENTERS?

Before "Remain in Mexico," in 2013 and 2014, Crystal Massey volunteered with an immigration lawyer in El Paso. She helped translate information and documents for people who were seeking asylum in the United States. Most of the clients were from Mexico, Guatemala, Honduras, and El Salvador.

As Crystal began to understand the complex asylum-seeking process, she was able to meet asylum seekers in Ciudad Juárez. She guided them through the legal processes and helped prepare their documentation about the danger they hoped to leave behind – the process to show credible fear. Then she escorted them to the border stations where they would formally ask for asylum. By law, they would be registered in the immigration system to evaluate the credibility of their case for protection. Crystal often had to present legal documentation that reminded reluctant border authorities of their obligation to assist individuals who ask for asylum.

Once they went through the border reviews, they were given restricted legal status in the United States as an asylum seeker. They were permitted to live with relatives or sponsors while they continued the extensive legal processes through the U.S. immigration courts. They were monitored by the immigration authorities, and it was rare that a person did not show up for their court appointments. That cost the government less than $5.00 per day.

Various sources cite the daily cost for housing immigrants in detention facilities. The calculations vary from about $150 to $500 per day.

With the changes in immigration policies created by

the Trump administration, more and more rights for asylum seekers were stripped. They were immediately placed in detention and not allowed to stay with sponsors and family. Now Crystal could not meet the asylum seekers; she never had a chance to assist them.

Some 100 expensive, government-funded detention centers, similar to jails, are located across the country, mostly in remote areas where social or legal services are hard to find. Many of these facilities are run by corporations that also manage the nation's private prisons. They are funded to a great extent by the United States government – citizens' tax dollars. As of the summer of 2020, about 50,000 immigrants were housed in these detention centers. The taxpayer expense is near $2.7 billion.[20]

One of those detention centers, South Texas Family Residential Center, was in Dilley, Texas. Crystal moved to that remote and hot little community a few hours from San Antonio, and fifteen hours from her husband and son. Volunteering there for most of a year, she helped provide and train other volunteers who would assist asylum seekers to catch that tiny window of access to provide humanitarian and legal care to the people in the detention center.

These asylum seekers had been through hellish experiences in their own countries, a perilous journey to the border, and now were locked in a haphazard detention

---

[20] American Immigration Council. Immigration Detention in the United States by Agency. Retrieved August 1, 2020, from https://www.americanimmigrationcouncil.org/sites/default/files/research/immigration_detention_in_the_united_states_by_agency.pdf

facility not designed for families who were confused and hurting. There were reports of unsanitary and unhealthy conditions. Very few had success in their petition for asylum. Many of these detainees, as of late 2020, were awaiting processing; more were deported. Some were held in detention for more than a year.

U.S. RESIDENTS, UNDOCUMENTED, DETAINED, AND DEPORTED

Along with the asylum seekers in the detention facilities are thousands of people who have been living in the United States without legal documentation. Border enforcement officers and sometimes local law enforcement are rewarded for finding "illegals" and arresting them. They are held in these detention centers – not official prisons, but yes, prisons – awaiting a hearing with a judge (an empty hope) or deportation orders. Most have no criminal convictions. The Journal of Crime and Justice published a research article that analyzed crime data over years showing that immigrant criminality is consistently lower than criminality of those born in the United States. Undocumented immigrants commit less property crimes, larceny, and burglary. There is little difference between the two groups for violent crime.[21]

Early in his term, President Trump authorized

---

[21] Robert M. Adelman, Yulin Yang, Lesley Williams Reid, James D. Bachmeier, & Mike Maciag. Using Estimates of Undocumented Immigrants to Study the Immigration-Crime Relationship. *Journal of Crime and Justice*, 2000.

thousands of law enforcement officers to search for and deport people who were living in the United States without documentation. Previous presidents have also implemented these practices. President Trump elevated the attacks.

The film series *Immigration Nation*, released in 2020, documented a collection of actual law enforcement actions to locate and deport people. The cameras followed officials as they hunted for and arrested the undocumented people. The actions shown on the screen include blatant violations of civil rights; often laughing at or ridiculing the people whose lives they are lacerating. It is evident that many officials believe that these Latin Americans who are living in the United States, working, and contributing to their communities, are a dangerous enemy. Some were veterans who had served the United States military. The officers repeatedly defend their actions, saying things like "This is just my job. I am following orders."

Many U.S. households are a mixture of U.S. citizens and residents who are in the United States without proper documentation. Those families stay in the shadows – fearing and avoiding anything that might bring government attention such as census counts, health care, reporting crimes, travel, and sometimes even schooling.

An example, one of millions, are my friends; we'll call them Maria and Marco. They married in Mexico and crossed into the United States in the late 1990s. Like so many others, they were fleeing extreme poverty and the violence that accompanies that poverty. Marco is a hard worker and has filled a need in New Mexico for heavy labor in construction. They have three children who are in school and doing well. Maria is working on a community college certificate. She dreams of becoming a preschool teacher. "This is why we came here, so our children will have a good education. I know that I cannot work when I get my certificate. That makes me sad. But my children will have a good future."

When I visit Maria, I call her as I approach her home. If she sees my car, she will open the door when I knock. "I know *La Migra* will come here someday. I have to keep the door locked. If they take us, my children will be alone." As she told me this, she was crying with heavy sobs. We arranged paperwork so that a trusted friend would have power of attorney over the children to care for them if that horrible day arrives. The friend's contact information is on speed dial in the children's phones, and they live every moment under a sky of fear.

~ 11 ~

THE WEIGHT OF HATE

In the first chapter, I shared a few of the problems I have caused in Mexico as I approached these new friends, as I was stretching to cross that cultural crevasse formed by the unequal distribution of wealth and power that has privileged me and disadvantaged them. My White privilege failed me there, restricting my ability to fully enjoy and learn from my sisters across the dry river. The women's gentleness and patience helped me across and showed me levels of oppression and acts of courage that I could never see on my own. I crave their extraordinary power to elevate their families and communities to levels of virtue. Now I understand better.

There exists in my culture a will to ignore the true stories of those south of this social chasm. Delving into factual accounts from the border and studying the immigration context is less attractive than that enormous, frosted cupcake, topped with sparkly things and exciting adventures that U.S. wealth provides. It is simpler to believe "those people" are murders and rapists. Block the border. Problem solved. Nothing for me to worry about.

Even more dangerous, however, are those who know more of the context, yet elevate their White Privilege to White Supremacy, and they base that in hate and violence.

VIOLENCE BORN OF CONVICTION

With the express purpose of eliminating hope for immigrants, early in his presidency Donald Trump spent billions of Americans' dollars to tighten border security and enforcement, to build some new walls along the Mexican border, to reinforce existing walls, and to implement a string of changes designed to severely constrain immigration. His border policing agencies were well-funded – $9.2 billion in 2003 rising to $24.7 billion in 2019. Previous presidents have also implemented harsh restrictions on immigration, mostly at the southern border; however, the Trump administration was most aggressive. These actions were based on blatant racism.

As mentioned earlier, Sonia Shah's[22] book, *The Next Great Migration*, provides an interesting look at the history of immigration experiences of humans as well as natural movement of plants and animals. She documents historical events and political thought that led Mr. Trump and his colleagues to implement these unbending and unprecedented measures. Much of the following information draws from Shah's accounts.

As conflicts bring turmoil, people flee their broken societies and dangerous conditions to enter more stable countries. In the receiving countries, anger toward immigrants escalates along with the fear, a grossly unfounded fear, that the immigrants will take our jobs and land, will corrupt our schools, and threaten our faith. We do acknowledge, of course, that real conflict can occur

---

[22] Sonia Shah (2020). *The Next Great Migration: The Beauty and Terror of Life on the Move*. Bloomsbury: New York.

between extreme overcrowding and the basic resources needed to survive. However, that level of extreme overcrowding in human communities is not common, especially in Europe and the United States.

Ignorance and unfounded fear elevate hostilities. And much of that fear stems from a feeling of innate superiority that can infest a society. In the early 1900s, a branch of the science community in Western cultures, seeking to substantiate White superiority, hosted literature and flawed studies reporting that, based on physical distinctions, there were five different human species which evolved from different sources; the White Western species of humans was superior. The term "race" was applied, touting a White superior race.

Race is not a biological distinction. Humans display characteristics that slide along thousands of continua that defy categorization including appearances as well as inherited and learned actions. Human DNA sequence in the genes themselves reveals the undeniable evidence that all groups of humans descended from a common ancestor, and that descent was relatively recent – some 200,000 years ago. All humans today are the same species, and there are no distinct races of humans.

However, the out-of-date and debunked superior White race theory and the crippling fear it generates resurfaced in the United States.

In 1979, John Tanton started the Federation for American Immigration Reform, designed specifically to restrict immigration. Others joined him and created similar organizations with the same anti-immigration goal, organizations such as the Center for Immigration Studies and NumbersUSA. The stated claim for their efforts was to slow population growth in the United States. Underneath, however, was Tanton's statement that foreigners are a "lasciviously breeding subspecies." White supremacists quickly aligned with these efforts hoping to increase their dwindling political power. The Southern Poverty Law Center designates Tanton's organizations as hate groups.

The Trump administration drew from employees and associates of Tanton's organizations to lead his immigration policies: Steve Bannon, Julie Kirchner, Kris Kobach, Kellyanne Conway, and Stephen Miller, a young man with little legal expertise or political experience who became advisor to the president on immigration policies. A colleague of Miller, Katie McHugh, described him as a White supremacist who fears that people from other cultures are coming to kill the White people. She collected some 900 emails from Stephen Miller, words full of fear and hatred for people of color and sent them to Southern Poverty Law Center's reporter Michael Edison Hayden.[23] He published a summary of these emails on the Southern Poverty Law Center's Hate Watch. Some of the content of those emails evidence extreme racism and are disturbing to read as they revealed Miller's long history of spreading hate-filled and fear-filled misinformation claiming that non-White people have organized to take over the country and to eventually eliminate White people.

---

[23] Michael Edison Hayden. Nov. 12, 2019. Stephen Miller White Nationalism Xenophobia Leaked in Emails. Southern Poverty Law Center Hate Watch. Retrieved September 30, 2020, from https://www.splcenter.org/hatewatch/2019/11/12/stephen-millers-affinity-white-nationalism-revealed-leaked-emails#link

Jean Guerrero's book,[24] *Hatemonger: Stephen Miller, Donald Trump, and the White Nationalist Agenda,* is based on some 150 interviews with people who knew and worked with Miller. She shows his advocating that the country is in grave danger of being overwhelmed by non-White peoples. Miller has been one of the few advisors to President Trump to remain in service. He encouraged a hatred of Americans who promote policies that are inclusive of non-White ethnic groups; they would "pollute" the White gene pool. It was Stephen Miller's advice that led to some of the harshest policies such as removing green cards, blocking the borders, and separating children from their families at the border – actions that meet technical definitions for kidnapping and torture. Stephen Miller remained on government payroll as a Trump advisor after he lost the presidency.

If we project behavior based in a belief that one "species" of human is superior, onto a worldwide screen, the horrors of racial divides, civil wars, and genocides come into focus. Hitler convinced his economically wounded citizens that the cause of their troubles was the "racially inferior" Jew. He instilled a hatred so strong that good citizens quickly turned into torturing and murdering monsters – the largest genocide in recent history. But that is just a portion of genocides in the 20th century, all causing hundreds of thousands of deaths: the Khmer Rouge's slaughter of Cambodians, the German siege of Leningrad, the slaughter of Tutsis in Rwanda, the mass

---

[24] Jean Guerrero. (2020). *Hate Monger, Stephen Miller, Donald Trump, and the White Nationalist Agenda.* William Morrow/HarperCollins: NY.

killing of Armenians and Greeks in Turkey, and the racist attacks on the Maya in Guatemala and indigenous tribes in Brazil. Wikipedia provides a much longer, sorrow-filled list under the topic "genocides by death toll."

Religious beliefs contribute to this hatred. Religious-based actions can strengthen altruism as we have seen in the women's stories, bringing peace and goodness to a harsh world. Many religious organizations, however, prioritize their religious creeds above the creeds of other religions. Allegiance to one idea of God empowers the followers to hate, harm, or kill those who follow a different idea of God. It can be extreme as seen in genocides, or subtle, as religions wall themselves in their own culture, closing their lives and minds to knowing and loving others.

Slanted and invented news reporting also contributes to the hatred by sensationalizing the immigrant experience and painting darker-skinned immigrants as evil criminals. Isolated stories of anecdotal data and false or twisted statistics with Stephen Miller-like context set that hatred in stone.

Mexican writer Octavio Paz[25] warns that conviction can become a concrete zeal, imposed with violence, thus leading to terrorism. "Terrorism obeys the same rules. It begins with the persecution of isolated groups – races, classes, dissenters, suspects – until gradually it touches everyone...a part of society regards the extermination of other groups with indifference, or even contributes." Time passes, power swings to a different extreme, and "the

---

[25] Octavio Paz. (1961). *The Labyrinth of Solitude: Life and Thought in Mexico*. Grove Press: NY.

persecutor is transformed into the persecuted. One turn of the political mechanism...and no one can escape this fierce dialect."

UNSTABLE SKIES

The United States started as immigrants invading, robbing, raping, enslaving, and killing the original peoples. When the invaders became the dominant culture, they imported, violently, immigrants whom they, again, robbed, raped, enslaved, and killed. Eventually, the nation's citizens divided themselves on this issue – on one side were those who welcomed immigrants with humane respect, and, on the other side, those who viewed immigrants as villains deserving abuse. That divide has persisted throughout history with the dominant voices heaving political actions and the immigrant experience to and fro.

This is not a call for open borders. Obviously, there is a tremendous need for a comprehensive immigration policy in collaboration with other countries and based in deep understandings, such as political and economic reasons for immigration; a just process for people to prove credible fear; a balance of economic resources; and a humane integration of immigrants. The positive impact of immigration should be made more public. Getting to know true stories about immigrants and immigrant seekers may help dispel those long-held hatreds and fears.

Existing U.S. immigration policies provide a structure to manage immigration, although out of date, flawed, and full of gaps. Creating a more fair and manageable immigration program will take years. It may be impossible. Managing immigration will be an ongoing struggle.

Increasing climate extremes with ravishing storms, political unrest with the abuse it spurs, wars and conflicts, lack of jobs, and criminal drug gangs with their reign of terror all plague scores of countries. More and more desperate people will come to the southern border of the United States: desperate people fleeing for their lives, some criminals, some duped by criminals, some wanting to join family in the United States, and some just gambling for a better life. Vetting the applicants is an important part of the immigration system and that requires hundreds more immigration lawyers.

Hatred for the other is embedded in the human experience, causing uncountable wars and genocides spanning human history with harmful impact that leaves stains on most every culture group. Yet, world society, overall, has made progress toward more respectful interactions and patient understanding. That can give us hope. For now, love and hate dance on the thin U.S.-Mexico borderline.

"Where you live correlates with nearly every major indicator of health and well-being, from the quality of education you receive to the kind of job you get to the health care your family can access. It determines what you eat, how far you commute, and how much you pay for government services."[26]

---

[26] *The Texas Observer*. The Gentrification of Texas. Retrieved May 2, 2020, from https://www.texasobserver.org/gentrification-texas-housing-special-issue/

RESOURCES

Below is a partial list of non-profit organizations whose work to support immigrant rights and whose media reports provided valuable insight for the book:

Mexico Solidarity Network
Center for Migration Studies
American Immigration Council
Save the Children Action Network
Border Servants Corp at Peace Lutheran Church
Center for Migration Studies
Evangelical Lutheran Church in America –
Accompanying Migrant Minors with Protection,
    Advocacy, Representation and Opportunities
    (AMMPARO)
International Association for Refugees
Junt@s Vamos
Seguimos Adelante
American Civil Liberties Union
Hope Border Institute
Catholic Legal Immigration Network, Inc.
Children Imprisoned at the Border 2018
Witness at the Border (formerly Witness: Tornillo)
Human Rights Watch
Lutheran Immigration and Refugee Service
Austin Tan Cerca de la Frontera

Centro Santa Catalina was started in Ciudad Juárez about 30 years ago by Dominican Sisters. Hundreds of women have learned skills (often sewing tablecloths and tote bags out of brightly colored oil cloth), advanced their education, and sustained their families.